SLOW COOKER

Recipe Book UK

CookNation

ISBN 978-1-913174-19-4

CONTENTS

The slow cooker

is your new best friend; an extremely economical and convenient method of cooking. They cook at lower temperatures than a traditional stove-top or oven method meaning you needn't worry about burning, boiling dry or over spills. The low temperature settings make it cheaper to run, even though it can be cooking for hours and the results deliver incredibly tender meats, even for cheaper cuts. Perhaps the best part of using a slow cooker is the time saving element. Other than basic preparation, you can leave the dish for hours to cook away while you get on with your day – perfect for busy people.

Using our collection of easy, no fuss, healthy recipes you can create stress-free, delicious, low calorie meals for the whole family. With **200** recipes to choose from there is something to please everyone and each is **calorie counted to under 200, 300, 400, 500 or 600 calories per serving** meaning you can also keep track of your daily food intake as you cook. The recipes can easily be 'bulked up' to include sides such as rice and potatoes if you're cooking for more people.

It's not just casseroles and stews that can be made in a slow cooker, as delicious as they are. You can make tasty soups, curries, snacks and desserts too.

The recipes are gathered into convenient sections to help you quickly find what you're looking for:

- Soups
- Family Favourites
- Casseroles & Stews
- Risottos
- Curries
- Seafood
- Vegetarian/Plant-based
- Gluten Free
- 5 Ingredients
- Snacks
- Desserts

Helpful things to note about our recipes

The recipes generally make between 4-6 servings and most take no longer than 15 mins to prepare.

All calorie information is on a per serving basis.

You will notice that ingredients regularly include items such as low cal spray or low cal/low fat butter spread. This is because using traditional cooking oils or full fat butter hugely increase the number of calories per serving. If you prefer not to prepare a 'skinny' recipe as stated, feel free to replace any lower calories items with ones of your choice.

Many of our recipes offer optional serving suggestions which are helpful when cooking for family or friends. For example serving with rice, pasta or potatoes. These are additional servings that are not included in the recipe calorie count. If you choose to include these, please be aware that you will need to allow for the additional calories if you are on a diet.

Slow cookers do not brown meat and while browning will make a difference to the taste of your recipe, if you really don't have the time, don't worry - it will still taste great.

All meat and vegetables should be cut into even sized pieces unless stated in the recipe. Some ingredients can take longer to cook than others, particularly root vegetables, but this has been allowed for in the cooking time.

Meat should be trimmed of visible fat and the skin removed unless stated otherwise.

Recipes can be divided and frozen into batches after cooling.

All the recipes in this book are a guide only. You may need to alter quantities and cooking times to suit your own appliances.

Curries - traditionally side dishes of bread and rice can be 'loaded' with calories so to follow are more calorie-conscious options to compliment our curries:

Each curry side suggestion serves 4
- 200g/7oz basmati rice 140 calories per serving
- 200g/7oz fine egg noodles 120 calories per serving
- 300g/11oz plain green salad 15 calories
- 200g/7oz cauliflower rice 50 calories per serving

To make cauliflower rice:
- Take one large cauliflower head (approximately 800g) and split into florets.
- Place into a food processor and 'whizz' until the cauliflower is the size of rice grains.
- Place the 'rice' in a microwaveable dish and cook covered for 4-5 minutes or until the piping hot.

5 Ingredients Recipes - If you're on a budget or low on fridge/store cupboard items, it is still possible to create delicious slow cooker meals with just 5 ingredients.

Many of our 5 ingredient recipes make use of 'hero' ingredients such as pesto or curry paste that are packed full of flavour and will really intensify the taste of your meal – they are also great time savers when you're prepping.

You will notice at first glance that many recipes appear to use more than 5 ingredients. This is because most recipes require key staples to cook. These basic items should always be in your store cupboard and therefore haven't been counted in the main 5 – you will most likely already have them:

- Salt & pepper
- Cooking oil spray
- Olive Oil
- Coconut oil
- Stock (Chicken, Beef, Vegetable, Fish)

Tips

- Our recipes have been tested using a 6.5 litre capacity slow cooker. You may need to adjust quantities and cooking times to suit your own appliance.
- All cooking times are a guide. Make sure you get to know your own slow cooker so that you can adjust timings accordingly.
- Read the manufacturers operating instructions as appliances can vary. For example, some recommend preheating the slow cooker for 20 minutes before use whilst others advocate switching on only when you are ready to start cooking.
- A spray of one calorie cooking oil in the cooker before adding ingredients will help with cleaning or you can buy slow cooker liners.
- Don't be tempted to regularly lift the lid of your appliance while cooking. The seal that is made with the lid on is all part of the slow cooking process. Each time you do lift the lid you will need to increase the cooking time.
- Removing the lid at the end of the cooking time can be useful to thicken up a sauce by adding additional cooking time and continuing to cook without the lid on. On the other hand if perhaps a sauce it too thick, removing the lid and adding a little more liquid can help.
- Always add hot liquids to your slow cooker, not cold.
- Do not overfill your slow cooker.
- Allow the inner dish of your slow cooker to completely cool before cleaning. Any stubborn marks can usually be removed after a period of soaking in hot soapy water.
- Be confident with your cooking. Feel free to use substitutes to suit your own taste and don't let a missing herb or spice stop you making a meal - you'll almost always be able to find something to replace it.

HOMEMADE STOCK

Homemade stock is not essential for any soup making, but you will find it can add additional depth of taste and further improve the flavour of some dishes.

Having said that, shop-bought stock has vastly improved in recent times and you may well decide that making your own stock isn't worth the time for the comparable result.

If you do use shop bought stock (which most people do) avoid buying budget options and anything too high in sodium.

For those of you who want to make stock from scratch, to follow are a few simple stock recipes to start with which you can quickly make on the stove-top.

Please note that all calorie information for each stock has already been accounted for in the soup recipes.

BASIC VEGETABLE STOCK

SERVES 4

- 1 tbsp olive oil
- 1 onion, chopped
- 1 leek, chopped
- 1 carrot, chopped
- 1 small bulb fennel, chopped
- 3 garlic cloves, crushed
- 1 tbsp black peppercorns
- 75g/3oz mushrooms
- 2 sticks celery, chopped
- 3 tomatoes, diced
- 2 tbsp freshly chopped flat leaf parsley
- 2 bay leaves
- 3lt/12 cups water

1 **Gently sauté the onions, leeks, carrots and fennel in the olive oil for a few minutes in a large lidded saucepan.**

2 **Add all the other ingredients, cover and bring to the boil. Leave to gently simmer for 20 minutes with the lid on.**

3 **Allow to cool for a little while.**

4 **Pour the contents through a sieve and store the finished stock liquid in the fridge for a couple of days or freeze in batches.**

BASIC CHICKEN STOCK

SERVES 4

- 1 tbsp olive oil
- 1 left over roast chicken carcass
- 2 carrots, chopped
- 2 onions, halved
- 2 stalks celery, chopped
- 10 black peppercorns
- 2 bay leaves
- 2 tbsp freshly chopped parsley
- 1 tsp freshly chopped thyme
- 3lt/12 cups water

1 Gently sauté the onions, leeks, carrots and fennel in the olive oil for a few minutes in a large lidded saucepan.

2 Add all the other ingredients, cover and bring to the boil. Leave to gently simmer for 20 minutes with the lid on.

3 Allow to cool for a little while.

4 Pour the contents through a sieve and store the finished stock liquid in the fridge for a couple of days or freeze in batches.

BASIC FISH STOCK

SERVES 4

- 1 tbsp olive oil
- 450g/1lb fish bones, heads carcasses etc (avoid oily fish when making stock)
- 4 leeks, chopped
- 1 fennel bulb, chopped
- 4 carrots, chopped
- 2 tbsp freshly chopped parsley
- 250ml/1 cup dry white wine
- 2.5lt/10 cups water

1 Gently sauté the carrots, leeks and fennel in the olive oil for a few minutes in a large lidded saucepan.

2 Clean the fish bones to ensure there is no blood as this can 'spoil' the stock.

3 Add all the other ingredients, cover and bring to the boil. Leave to very gently simmer for 1hr with the lid on.

4 Allow to cool for a little while.

5 Pour the contents through a sieve and store the finished stock liquid in the fridge for a couple of days or freeze in batches.

6 You may find you need to skim a little fat from the top of the stock after cooking.

BEETROOT SOUP

SERVES 4   CALORIES PER SERVING 160

- 1 onion, chopped
- 1 tsp cumin seeds
- 150g/5oz potatoes, chopped
- 400g/14oz beetroot, cubed
- 750ml/3 cups vegetable stock
- 1 tsp dried basil or oregano
- 1 tsp lemon juice
- 4 tbsp fat free Greek yoghurt
- Salt & pepper to taste
- Low cal cooking oil spray

1 Preheat the slow cooker while you prepare the ingredients.

2 Gently sauté the onion & cumin seeds in a little low cal oil for a few minutes until the onions soften.

3 Add all the ingredients to the slow cooker, except the Greek yoghurt. Combine well, cover and leave to cook on high for 1-1½ hours or until the vegetables are cooked through.

4 Blend to a smooth consistency.

5 Check the seasoning and serve with a dollop of yoghurt in the middle of each bowl.

This soup has a fantastic vibrant colour, which is contrasted by a generous dollop of white yoghurt.

THREE BEAN SOUP

SERVES 4   CALORIES PER SERVING 230

- 2 leeks, sliced
- 1 onion, sliced
- 2 garlic cloves, crushed
- 1 carrot, chopped
- 1 green chilli, finely chopped
- 400g/14oz tinned mixed beans, drained
- 125g/4oz courgettes, sliced
- 2 tbsp tomato puree/paste
- 1lt/4 cups vegetable stock
- Salt & pepper to taste
- Low cal cooking oil spray

1 Preheat the slow cooker while you prepare the ingredients.

2 Gently sauté the leeks, onion & garlic in a little low cal oil for a few minutes until softened.

3 Add all the ingredients to the slow cooker. Combine well, cover and leave to cook on high for 1-1½ hours or until the vegetables are cooked through.

4 Check the seasoning and serve.

If you don't have fresh chillies, use a little chilli powder or cayenne pepper.

SIMPLE LENTIL SOUP

SERVES 4 | CALORIES PER SERVING 220

- 1 onion, chopped
- 2 celery sticks, chopped
- 2 garlic cloves, crushed
- 1 carrot, chopped
- 225g/8oz red lentils
- 1 bay leaf
- 1lt/4 cups vegetable stock
- 4 tsp low fat crème fraiche
- Salt & pepper to taste
- Low cal cooking oil spray

1 Preheat the slow cooker while you prepare the ingredients.

2 Gently sauté the onion, celery & garlic in a little low cal oil for a few minutes until the onions soften.

3 Add all the ingredients to the slow cooker, except the crème fraiche. Combine well, cover and leave to cook on high for 1-2 hours or until the vegetables are cooked through and the lentils are tender.

4 Remove the bay leaf and blend the soup to a smooth consistency.

5 Check the seasoning and serve with a tsp of crème fraiche in the middle of each bowl.

You could garnish with freshly chopped coriander or flat leaf parsley if you have it to hand.

SPLIT PEA SOUP

SERVES 4 | CALORIES PER SERVING 230

- 2 onions, chopped
- 2 celery sticks, chopped
- 2 garlic cloves, crushed
- 2 carrots, chopped
- 1 turnip, chopped
- 225g/8oz pre-soaked yellow split peas
- 2 tsp mixed dried herbs
- 1lt/4 cups vegetable stock
- Salt & pepper to taste
- Low cal cooking oil spray

1 Preheat the slow cooker while you prepare the ingredients.

2 Gently sauté the onion, celery & garlic in a little low cal oil for a few minutes until the onions soften.

3 Add all the ingredients to the slow cooker. Combine well, cover and leave to cook on high for 1-2 hours or until the vegetables are cooked through and the split peas are tender.

4 Blend the soup to a smooth consistency, season and serve.

Thyme, basil or oregano will all work in this soup if you don't have dried mixed herbs.

PEA & MINT SOUP

SERVES 4 CALORIES PER SERVING 200

- 2 onions, chopped
- 2 garlic cloves, crushed
- 200g/7oz potatoes, chopped
- 1 tsp medium curry powder
- 500g/1lb 2oz peas
- 3 tbsp freshly chopped mint
- 750ml/3 cups vegetable stock
- 250ml/1 cup semi skimmed/half fat milk
- Salt & pepper to taste
- Low cal cooking oil spray

1 Preheat the slow cooker while you prepare the ingredients.

2 Gently sauté the onion & garlic in a little low cal oil for a few minutes until the onions soften.

3 Add all the ingredients to the slow cooker. Combine well, cover and leave to cook on high for 1-1½ hours or until the vegetables are tender.

4 Blend the soup to a smooth consistency, season and serve.

Reserve a little of the chopped mint as a garnish.

SWEET POTATO & ORANGE SOUP

SERVES 4 CALORIES PER SERVING 190

- 2 onions, chopped
- 2 carrots, chopped
- 500g/1lb 2oz sweet potatoes, chopped
- 750ml/3 cups vegetable stock
- 250ml/1 cup fresh orange juice
- Salt & pepper to taste
- Low cal cooking oil spray

1 Preheat the slow cooker while you prepare the ingredients.

2 Gently sauté the onion in a little low cal oil for a few minutes until softened.

3 Add all the ingredients to the slow cooker. Combine well, cover and leave to cook on high for 1-1½ hours or until the vegetables are tender.

4 Blend the soup to a smooth consistency, season and serve.

Freshly chopped coriander makes a really worthwhile addition to this soup.

HONEY & CARROT SOUP

- SERVES 4
- CALORIES PER SERVING 130

- 1 onion, chopped
- 500g/1lb 2oz carrots, chopped
- 125g/4oz potatoes, chopped
- 1lt/4 cups vegetable stock
- 1 tsp runny honey
- Salt & pepper to taste
- Low cal cooking oil spray

1 Preheat the slow cooker while you prepare the ingredients.

2 Gently sauté the onions in a little low cal oil for a few minutes until softened.

3 Add all the ingredients to the slow cooker. Combine well, cover and leave to cook on high for 1-1½ hours or until the vegetables are tender.

4 Blend the soup to a smooth consistency, season and serve.

Freshly chopped chives and/or a swirl of single cream make a lovely garnish to this soup.

CURRIED POTATO SOUP

- SERVES 4
- CALORIES PER SERVING 180

- 1 onion, chopped
- 2 garlic cloves, crushed
- 1 tbsp medium curry powder
- 400g/14oz potatoes, peeled & cut into chunks
- 200g/7oz peas
- 1lt/4 cups vegetable stock
- 3 tbsp fat free Greek yoghurt
- Lemon wedges to serve
- Salt & pepper to taste
- Low cal cooking oil spray

1 Preheat the slow cooker while you prepare the ingredients.

2 Gently sauté the onion & garlic in a little low cal oil for a few minutes until softened.

3 Add all the ingredients to the slow cooker, except the Greek yoghurt. Combine well, cover and leave to cook on high for 1-1½ hours or until the potatoes are tender but not completely falling apart.

4 Remove 2 ladles of soup and use a blender to blend this to a smooth consistency. Return the blended portion to the rest of the soup.

5 Stir through the yoghurt, combine well, season and serve.

Finely chopped red chillies make a good garnish for this soup if you want to add additional 'heat'.

CREAMY MUSHROOM SOUP

SERVES 4 CALORIES PER SERVING 140

- 1 onion, chopped
- ½ tsp nutmeg
- 125g/4oz potatoes, chopped
- 500g/1lb 2oz mushrooms, sliced
- 750ml/3 cups vegetable stock
- 250ml/1 cup semi skimmed/half fat milk
- 4 tsp low fat crème fraiche
- Salt & pepper to taste
- Low cal cooking oil spray

1 Preheat the slow cooker while you prepare the ingredients.

2 Gently sauté the onions in a little low cal oil for a few minutes until softened.

3 Add all the ingredients to the slow cooker, except the crème fraiche. Combine well, cover and leave to cook on high for 1-1½ hours or until the potatoes are tender.

4 Blend the soup to a smooth consistency.

5 Season and serve with a teaspoon of crème fraiche stirred through each bowl.

Freshly chopped tarragon or chives make a good garnish for this soup.

ONION & SQUASH SOUP

SERVES 4 CALORIES PER SERVING 150

- 2 onions, chopped
- 2 garlic cloves, crushed
- 1 carrot, chopped
- 1 carrot, finely grated
- 500g/1lb 2oz butternut squash flesh, diced
- 1lt/4 cups vegetable stock
- Salt & pepper to taste
- Low cal cooking oil spray

1 Preheat the slow cooker while you prepare the ingredients.

2 Gently sauté the onion & garlic in a little low cal oil for a few minutes until the onions soften.

3 Add all the ingredients to the slow cooker, except the grated carrot. Combine well, cover and leave to cook on high for 1-1½ hours or until the vegetables are tender.

4 Blend the soup to a smooth consistency.

5 Season and serve with the grated carrot on top.

Freshly chopped chives make a good garnish for this soup.

TOMATO SOUP

- SERVES 4
- CALORIES PER SERVING 165

- 1 onion, chopped
- 2 garlic cloves, crushed
- 200g/7oz potatoes, chopped
- 200g/7oz fresh ripe tomatoes, chopped
- 400g/14oz tinned chopped tomatoes
- 1 tsp dried basil
- ½ tsp salt
- 1 tsp brown sugar
- 250ml/1 cup vegetable stock
- Salt & pepper to taste
- Low cal cooking oil spray

1 Preheat the slow cooker while you prepare the ingredients.

2 Gently sauté the onion & garlic in a little low cal oil for a few minutes until the onions soften.

3 Add all the ingredients to the slow cooker. Combine well, cover and leave to cook on high for 1-1½ hours or until the vegetables are tender.

4 Blend the soup to a smooth consistency, season and serve.

The salt and sugar will help balance the acidity of the tomatoes. Use a little more if needed.

SIMPLE MINESTRONE SOUP

- SERVES 4
- CALORIES PER SERVING 200

- 1 onion, chopped
- 2 celery sticks, finely chopped
- 2 carrots, finely chopped
- 400g/14oz tinned chopped tomatoes
- 75g/3oz dried spaghetti, roughly broken up
- 1lt/4 cups vegetable stock
- 2 tbsp freshly grated Parmesan cheese
- Salt & pepper to taste
- Low cal cooking oil spray

1 Preheat the slow cooker while you prepare the ingredients.

2 Gently sauté the onion & celery in a little low cal oil for a few minutes until the onions soften.

3 Add all the ingredients to the slow cooker, except the grated Parmesan cheese. Combine well, cover and leave to cook on high for 1-1½ hours or until the vegetables & pasta are tender.

4 Season and serve with Parmesan sprinkled over the top.

Any type of small pasta shapes will work fine for this simple minestrone style soup.

CLASSIC CHICKEN SOUP

SERVES 4 CALORIES PER SERVING 140

- 2 onions, chopped
- 2 carrots, finely chopped
- 2 sticks celery, finely chopped
- 350g/12oz cooked chicken breast, shredded
- 2 garlic cloves, crushed
- 1lt/4 cups chicken stock
- Salt & pepper to taste
- Low cal cooking oil spray

1 Preheat the slow cooker while you prepare the ingredients.

2 Gently sauté the onions, carrots, celery & garlic in a little low cal oil for a few minutes until the onions soften.

3 Add all the ingredients to the slow cooker. Combine well, cover and leave to cook on high for 1-1½ hours or until the vegetables are tender.

4 Remove 2 ladles of soup and use a blender to blend this to a smooth consistency. Return the blended portion of the soup to the rest of the soup.

5 Stir well, season and serve.

Chicken soup is traditionally made with left over shredded chicken. This version uses the leanest cut of the bird - breast meat. Other cuts will have a higher fat content.

CHICKEN & FRESH ASPARAGUS SOUP

SERVES 4 CALORIES PER SERVING 190

- 1 onion, chopped
- 2 garlic cloves, crushed
- 350g/12oz skinless chicken breast, finely sliced
- 50g/2oz fine rice noodles
- 120ml/½ cup dry white wine
- 1lt/4 cups chicken stock
- 200g/7oz fresh asparagus tips, roughly chopped
- 1 small bunch spring onions, finely sliced lengthways
- Salt & pepper to taste
- Low cal cooking oil spray

1 Preheat the slow cooker while you prepare the ingredients.

2 Gently sauté the onion & garlic in a little low cal oil for a few minutes until the onions soften.

3 Add all the ingredients to the slow cooker, except the asparagus & spring onions. Combine well, cover and leave to cook on high for 1½ hours.

4 Add the asparagus and cook for a further 10-20 minutes or until the chicken is cooked through and the asparagus is tender but not overcooked.

5 Sprinkle with sliced spring onions, season and serve.

Adding the asparagus towards the end of the cooking time should ensure it still has a little crunch. Feel free to add at the beginning if you prefer it super-tender.

CHICKEN & LEEK SOUP

SERVES 4 · CALORIES PER SERVING 140

- 1 onion, chopped
- 2 garlic cloves, crushed
- 200g/7oz skinless chicken breast, chopped
- 200g/7oz leeks, sliced
- 1lt/4 cups chicken stock
- 125g/4oz potatoes, chopped
- 1 tsp dried basil or oregano
- Salt & pepper to taste
- Low cal cooking oil spray

1 Preheat the slow cooker while you prepare the ingredients.

2 Gently sauté the onions, garlic & chicken in a little low cal oil for a few minutes until the onions soften.

3 Add all the ingredients to the slow cooker. Combine well, cover and leave to cook on high for 1½-2 hours or until the chicken is cooked through and the potatoes are tender.

4 Use a blender to blend the soup to your preferred consistency.

5 Season and serve.

You could also add some chopped pitted prunes to this soup for a different twist.

ASIAN CHICKEN & RICE SOUP

SERVES 4 · CALORIES PER SERVING 230

- 1 onion, chopped
- 2 garlic cloves, crushed
- 2 carrots, sliced lengthways
- 200g/7oz skinless chicken breast, chopped
- 2 tbsp tomato puree/paste
- 1lt/4 cups chicken stock
- 200g/7oz basmati rice
- 60ml/¼ cup fresh orange juice
- 1 tsp dried basil or chives
- Salt & pepper to taste
- Low cal cooking oil spray

1 Preheat the slow cooker while you prepare the ingredients.

2 Gently sauté the onion & garlic in a little low cal oil for a few minutes until the onions soften.

3 Add all the ingredients to the slow cooker, except the orange juice. Combine well, cover and leave to cook on high for 1½-2 hours or until the chicken is cooked through.

4 Remove 2 ladles of soup and use a blender to blend this to a smooth consistency. Return the blended portion to the rest of the soup.

5 Add the orange juice, combine well, season and serve.

Freshly chopped chives make a great garnish for this soup.

CHICKEN & PASTA SOUP

SERVES 4   CALORIES PER SERVING 240

- 1 onion, chopped
- 2 garlic cloves, crushed
- 2 carrots, sliced lengthways
- 300g/11oz skinless chicken breast, chopped
- 150g/5oz soup pasta
- 2 tsp dried mixed herbs
- 750ml/3 cups chicken stock
- Salt & pepper to taste
- Low cal cooking oil spray

1 Preheat the slow cooker while you prepare the ingredients.

2 Gently sauté the onion & garlic in a little low cal oil for a few minutes until the onions soften.

3 Add all the ingredients to the slow cooker. Combine well, cover and leave to cook on high for 1½-2 hours or until the chicken is cooked through and the pasta is tender.

4 Season and serve.

Any type of small pasta shape will work for this soup. Add a little grated Parmesan cheese when serving if you wish.

CREAMY CHICKEN & CORN SOUP

SERVES 4   CALORIES PER SERVING 240

- 1 onion, chopped
- 125g/4oz potatoes, chopped
- 750ml/3 cups semi skimmed/half fat milk
- 250ml/1 cup chicken stock
- 200g/7oz skinless chicken breast, chopped
- 400g/14oz sweetcorn
- ½ tsp nutmeg
- 2 bay leaves
- Salt & pepper to taste
- Low cal cooking oil spray

1 Preheat the slow cooker while you prepare the ingredients.

2 Gently sauté the onion in a little low cal oil for a few minutes until softened.

3 Add all the ingredients to the slow cooker. Combine well, cover and leave to cook on high for 1½-2 hours or until the chicken is cooked through.

4 Discard the bay leaves.

5 Remove 2 ladles of soup and use a blender to blend this to a smooth consistency. Return the blended portion to the rest of the soup.

6 Combine well, season and serve.

You could garnish this soup with freshly chopped chives and a tablespoon of fat free Greek yoghurt.

BEEF & VEGETABLE BROTH

SERVES 4 · CALORIES PER SERVING 150

- 225g/8oz lean rump steak, finely sliced
- 1 leek, chopped
- 1 onion, chopped
- 2 garlic cloves, crushed
- 2 carrots, chopped
- 50g/2oz pre soaked pearl barley
- 2 celery sticks, chopped
- 1ltml/4 cups beef stock
- Salt & pepper to taste
- Low cal cooking oil spray

1 Preheat the slow cooker while you prepare the ingredients.

2 Gently sauté the leeks, onion & garlic in a little low cal oil for a few minutes until they soften.

3 Add all the ingredients to the slow cooker. Combine well, cover and leave to cook on high for 1½-2 hours or until the vegetables are tender and the steak is cooked through.

4 Check the seasoning and serve.

Any cut of beef steak will work fine for this recipe provided it's sliced thinly enough.

BEEF & BAMBOO SHOOT SOUP

SERVES 4 · CALORIES PER SERVING 190

- 225g/4oz lean rump steak, finely sliced
- 1 leek, chopped
- 1 onion, chopped
- 2 celery sticks, chopped
- 1 garlic clove, crushed
- 2 carrots, chopped
- 1 tbsp soy sauce
- 2 tbsp tomato puree/paste
- 75g/3oz long grain rice
- 125g/4oz tinned bamboo shoots
- 1ltml/4 cups beef stock
- Salt & pepper to taste
- Low cal cooking oil spray

1 Preheat the slow cooker while you prepare the ingredients.

2 Gently sauté the leeks, onion, celery & garlic in a little low cal oil for a few minutes until they soften.

3 Add all the ingredients to the slow cooker. Combine well, cover and leave to cook on high for 1½-2 hours or until the vegetables and rice are tender and the steak is cooked through.

4 Check the seasoning and serve.

Chopped fresh chives make a good garnish for this tasty soup.

PEA & HAM SOUP

SERVES 4 CALORIES PER SERVING 290

- 1 onion, chopped
- 2 garlic cloves, crushed
- 200g/7oz pre soaked yellow split peas
- 2 carrots, chopped
- 2 tsp dried mixed herbs
- 125g/4oz smoked ham or gammon, chopped
- 1lt/4 cups chicken stock
- Salt & pepper to taste
- Low cal cooking oil spray

1 Preheat the slow cooker while you prepare the ingredients.

2 Gently sauté the onion & garlic in a little low cal oil for a few minutes until the onions soften.

3 Add all the ingredients to the slow cooker. Combine well, cover and leave to cook on high for 1½-2 hours or until everything is tender.

4 Remove 2 ladles of soup and use a blender to blend this to a smooth consistency. Return the blended portion of the soup to the rest of the soup.

5 Combine well, season and serve.

Lean ham stripped from a smoked ham hock is ideal for this recipe, but you can use whatever you have to hand.

ASIAN PORK SOUP

SERVES 4 CALORIES PER SERVING 145

- 1 onion, chopped
- 2 garlic cloves, crushed
- 125g/4oz pork tenderloin, chopped
- 2 carrots, sliced lengthways
- 1 bunch spring onions, sliced lengthways
- 2 tbsp soy sauce
- ½ tsp Chinese five spice powder
- 2 tbsp rice wine vinegar
- 1 red chilli, finely chopped
- 200g/7oz tinned water chestnuts
- 1lt/4 cups chicken stock
- Salt & pepper to taste
- Low cal cooking oil spray

1 Preheat the slow cooker while you prepare the ingredients.

2 Gently sauté the onion, garlic & pork in a little low cal oil for a few minutes until the onions soften.

3 Add all the ingredients to the slow cooker. Combine well, cover and leave to cook on high for 1-1½ hours or until the pork and vegetables are cooked through.

4 Season and serve.

Cooked left-over pork is fine to use in this recipe too.

LENTIL & BACON SOUP

- SERVES 4
- CALORIES PER SERVING 270

- 1 onion, chopped
- 2 garlic cloves, crushed
- 125g/4oz lean back bacon, chopped
- 200g/7oz potatoes, chopped
- 225g/8oz red lentils
- 2 carrot, chopped
- 2 tsp dried mixed herbs
- 1lt/4 cups chicken stock
- Salt & pepper to taste
- Low cal cooking oil spray

1 Preheat the slow cooker while you prepare the ingredients.

2 Gently sauté the onion, garlic & bacon in a little low cal oil for a few minutes until the onions soften.

3 Add all the ingredients to the slow cooker. Combine well, cover and leave to cook on high for 1½-2 hours or until everything is tender and cooked through.

4 Remove 2 ladles of soup and use a blender to blend this to a smooth consistency. Return the blended portion of the soup to the rest of the soup.

5 Combine well, season and serve.

Streaky bacon is fine to use too, but it will have a higher fat content.

BEEF & NEW POTATO SOUP

- SERVES 4
- CALORIES PER SERVING 200

- 1 leek, chopped
- 1 onion, chopped
- 2 garlic cloves, crushed
- 2 celery sticks, chopped
- 2 carrots, sliced lengthways
- 200g/7oz baby new potatoes, halved
- 100g/4oz baby sweetcorn cobs, sliced lengthways
- 225g/8oz lean rump steak, finely sliced
- 1ltml/4 cups beef stock
- Salt & pepper to taste
- Low cal cooking oil spray

1 Preheat the slow cooker while you prepare the ingredients.

2 Gently sauté the leeks, onion, garlic & celery in a little low cal oil for a few minutes until they soften.

3 Add all the ingredients to the slow cooker. Combine well, cover and leave to cook on high for 1½-2 hours or until the potatoes and steak are tender and cooked through.

4 Check the seasoning and serve.

Any type of halved small or baby potatoes will work well for this recipe, but you could just use chunks of regular potatoes too.

BACON & BEAN SOUP

SERVES 4 · CALORIES PER SERVING 220

- 1 leek, chopped
- 1 onion, sliced
- 2 garlic cloves, crushed
- 2 celery stalks, chopped
- 125g/4oz lean back bacon, chopped
- 1 carrot, chopped
- 1 green chilli, finely chopped
- 400g/14oz tinned mixed beans, drained
- 2 tbsp tomato puree/paste
- 1lt/4 cups chicken stock
- Salt & pepper to taste
- Low cal cooking oil spray

1 Preheat the slow cooker while you prepare the ingredients.

2 Gently sauté the leeks, onions, garlic, celery & bacon in a little low cal oil for a few minutes until softened.

3 Add all the ingredients to the slow cooker. Combine well, cover and leave to cook on high for 1½-2 hours or until the vegetables and bacon are cooked through.

4 Check the seasoning and serve.

For an alternative twist try using sun-dried tomato puree/paste.

INDIAN LAMB & CHICKPEA SOUP

SERVES 4 · CALORIES PER SERVING 250

- 1 leek, chopped
- 1 onion, chopped
- 2 garlic cloves, crushed
- 200g/7oz lean lamb fillet, finely sliced
- 400g/14oz tinned chopped tomatoes
- 200g/7oz tinned chickpeas, drained
- 500ml/2 cups chicken stock
- 1 tbsp medium curry powder
- 1 red chilli, finely chopped
- Salt & pepper to taste
- Low cal cooking oil spray

1 Preheat the slow cooker while you prepare the ingredients.

2 Gently sauté the leeks, onions, garlic & lamb in a little low cal oil for a few minutes softened.

3 Add all the ingredients to the slow cooker, except the chopped chilli. Combine well, cover and leave to cook on high for 1½-2 hours or until the ingredients are cooked through and tender.

4 Check the seasoning and serve with the chopped chilli sprinkled on top.

Freshly chopped coriander makes a great garnish for this soup.

THAI CRAB SOUP

SERVES 4 CALORIES PER SERVING 210

- 400g/14oz tinned crab meat, drained
- 2 tbsp Thai red curry paste
- 750ml/3 cups chicken or fish stock
- 250ml/1 cup low fat coconut milk
- Small bunch spring onions, chopped
- Salt & pepper to taste
- Low cal cooking oil spray

1 Preheat the slow cooker while you prepare the ingredients.

2 Add all the ingredients to the slow cooker. Combine well, cover and leave to cook on high for 45mins-1 hour or until the soup is piping hot.

3 Season and serve.

You could use fresh crab meat and/or prawns in this soup along with freshly chopped coriander if you have it.

SMOKED HADDOCK SOUP

SERVES 4 CALORIES PER SERVING 230

- 300g/11oz skinless, boneless smoked haddock fillets, cubed
- 300g/11oz potatoes, peeled & cubed
- 1lt/4 cups semi skimmed/half fat milk
- 1 tsp low fat olive 'butter' spread
- Salt & pepper to taste
- Low cal cooking oil spray

1 Preheat the slow cooker while you prepare the ingredients.

2 Add all the ingredients to the slow cooker. Combine well, cover and leave to cook on high for 1-1½ hours or until the potatoes are tender and the fish is cooked through.

3 Remove 2 ladles of soup and use a blender to blend this to a smooth consistency. Return the blended portion to the rest of the soup.

4 Combine well, season and serve.

You could blend all the soup if you prefer a smooth consistency throughout.

HONEYED CHICKEN WINGS

SERVES 4 CALORIES PER SERVING 453

- 16 large skinless chicken wings
- 1 tsp freshly grated ginger (or ½ tsp ground ginger)
- 2 cloves garlic, crushed
- 1 tbsp runny honey
- 1 tbsp light soy sauce
- 1 tsp sesame oil
- 1 tbsp lemon juice
- 1 carrot peeled into ribbons
- 4 spring onions, chopped
- 120ml/½ cup stock
- 2 tsp sesame seeds
- Salt and pepper to taste

1 Coat the chicken wings in the runny honey and then combine with all the other ingredients, except the spring onions and sesame seeds, in the slow cooker. Leave to cook on high for approx 4 hours or low for 6 hours.

2 Serve sprinkled with the spring onions and sesame seeds.

This is a lovely sweet, tender chicken recipe which is great to share with family & friends.

TENDER WHOLE CHICKEN

SERVES 6 CALORIES PER SERVING 446

- 2kg/ 4½lb skinless whole chicken
- 2 onions, sliced into rings
- Dried rub mix of :
- 1 tsp each garlic powder, thyme, paprika & onion powder + pinch salt

1 Combine the dried ingredients together and rub really well into the fresh chicken.

2 Place the onions in the bottom of the slow cooker and put the chicken on top. Cook on low for 7-8 hours with the lid tightly shut. Ensure the chicken is cooked through.

3 Serve with your choice of vegetables, potatoes or salad.

Whole cooked chicken really comes into its own in the slow cooker. This super-simple recipe will give you the heart of a meal which, with leftovers, can last a couple of days.

BBQ CHICKEN

SERVES 4 — CALORIES PER SERVING 235

- 450g/1lb skinless chicken breasts
- 1 tsp each, smoked paprika & garlic powder
- 120ml/½ cup chicken stock
- ½ tsp each ground cumin & ground coriander
- 1 tbsp brown sugar
- 3 tbsp Worcestershire sauce or steak sauce
- ½ tsp salt
- 3 tbsp tomato puree/paste or ketchup

1 Put all the ingredients into the slow cooker. Mix well, cover and leave to cook on low for 4-5 hours or until the chicken is cooked through and tender.

2 Shred the chicken breasts with 2 forks and mix back into the sauce at the bottom of the slow cooker.

3 If the sauce needs to be thickened, continue to cook on high for up to 45 mins with the lid off. Alternatively if it's too sticky, add a little water to loosen up.

4 Serve with salad or in sandwich rolls with mayonnaise and BBQ sauce.

When the chicken is shredded and mixed back into the sauce, you should be left with a moist versatile mixture which is effectively the poultry version of the BBQ classic 'pulled pork'.

SIMPLE CHICKEN CURRY

SERVES 4 — CALORIES PER SERVING 223

- 500g/1lb 2oz skinless chicken breasts
- 1 onion, chopped
- 1 tbsp tomato puree/paste
- 3 cloves garlic, crushed
- 1 tsp low fat butter spread
- 1 tbsp fresh grated ginger (or use 1 tsp of ginger powder)
- 1 tsp garam masala
- 1 tsp ground cumin
- 1 tsp turmeric
- ½ tsp chilli powder
- 250ml/1 cup low fat Greek yoghurt
- 375ml/1 ½ cups passata/sieved tomatoes
- Salt & pepper to taste

1 Combine all the ingredients, except the yoghurt, into the slow cooker. Cook on low for 5-6 hours or on high for 3-4 hours with the lid tightly shut.

2 Ensure the chicken is cooked through and tender, turn off the heat and stir in the yoghurt.

3 Serve with green beans and naan bread.

The mix of spices suggested in the recipe is preferable but it is fine to substitute with curry powder if you are in a rush or struggling with store cupboard ingredients.

ITALIAN MEATBALLS

SERVES 5 CALORIES PER SERVING 323

- 650g/1lb 7oz lean, minced/ground beef
- 1 slice bread, whizzed into bread crumbs using a food processor
- ½ onion, finely chopped
- Handful fresh parsley, chopped
- 1 large free range egg
- 1 clove garlic, crushed
- ½ tsp salt
- 2 400g/14 oz tins chopped tomatoes
- 2 tbsp tomato puree/paste
- 250ml/1 cup beef stock
- 1 tsp each dried basil, oregano & thyme

1 Combine together the beef, breadcrumbs, egg, onion, garlic and half the salt. (You can do it with your hands or for super-speed put it all into a food mixer).

2 Once the ingredients are properly mixed together, use your hands to shape into approximately 20-24 meat balls.

3 Add all the ingredients to the slow cooker and combine well. Cover and leave to cook on low for 5-6 hours or 3-4 hours on high.

4 Ensure the beef is well cooked and serve with spaghetti, parmesan and a green salad.

Meatballs are easy to make and never a disappointment to eat. The simple sauce accompanying the meat here is lovely just as it is, but a dash of Worcestershire sauce or a teaspoon of marmite will give it additional depth.

CHILLI CON CARNE

SERVES 4 CALORIES PER SERVING 440

- 550g/1¼ lb lean, minced/ground beef
- 1 400g/14oz tin chopped tomatoes
- 1 400g/14oz tin kidney beans, drained
- 1 large onion, chopped
- 250ml/1 cup beef stock
- 250ml/1 cup tomato passata/sieved tomatoes
- 1 tsp each of brown sugar, oregano, cumin, chilli powder, paprika & garlic powder
- ½ tsp salt
- Low cal cooking spray

1 Brown the mince and onions in a frying pan. Add all the ingredients into the slow cooker and combine well. Leave to cook on low for 5-6 hours or high for 3-4 hours with the lid tightly closed.

2 Once the meat is fully cooked through, serve with rice or tortilla chips and a dollop of low fat yoghurt or crème fraiche.

The Spanish name simply means 'chilli with meat' and this dish has been a Tex-Mex classic since before the days of the American frontier settlers. Slow cooking the mince beef really allows the flavour to develop.

RAGU A LA BOLOGNESE

SERVES 4 · CALORIES PER SERVING 344

- 500g/1lb 2oz lean, minced/ground beef
- 1 400g/14oz tin chopped tomatoes
- 250ml/1 cup passata/sieved tomatoes
- 1 tsp each dried oregano & thyme
- 1 stick celery chopped
- 2 bay leaves
- 1 tbsp tomato puree/paste
- 3 garlic cloves, crushed
- 2 onions, chopped
- Salt and pepper to taste
- Low cal cooking spray

1 Quickly brown the meat in a frying pan with a little low cal spray. Combine all the ingredients in the slow cooker and close the lid tightly.

2 Leave to cook on low for 5-6 hours or high for 3-4 hours.

3 Make sure the meat is cooked through and serve with rigatoni, penne or spaghetti.

Nothing can be simpler or more satisfying than spaghetti bolognese. You can add mushrooms and peppers to the recipe if you like, plus a dash or two of Worcestershire sauce gives extra depth.

PERFECT PULLED PORK

SERVES 6 · CALORIES PER SERVING 280

- 900g/2lb pork butt (shoulder)
- 1 onion, chopped
- 250ml/1 cup BBQ sauce or ketchup
- 250ml/1 cup beef stock or boiling water
- 1 packet BBQ dry rub

Or make your own:

- 1 tbsp each of garlic powder, brown sugar, onion powder, celery salt, paprika + 1 tsp each mild chilli powder & cumin

1 Combine all the spices together and cover the pork in the dry spice rub. Add the stock, onion & BBQ sauce and then place the pork on top. Leave to cook on high for 6-8 hours with the lid tightly closed. Ideally you should turn the pork over half way through cooking, but if you can't do that don't worry.

2 Once the pork is tender remove it from the slow cooker. Leave to rest for as long as you can resist and then use your hands or 2 forks to pull the pork apart.

3 Once it's all shredded, place in a bowl and remove the cooking liquid from the slow cooker. Pour the liquid onto the pork to make beautiful, juicy meat.

4 Enjoy with just about everything, whether it's a light salad or sandwich rolls with BBQ sauce and salad.

Pulled pork is an absolute classic. It's a chance to use almost everything in your spice rack to create a 'killer' dry rub and it always packs an irresistible punchy and more-ish taste.

COWBOY CASSEROLE

SERVES 4 CALORIES PER SERVING 414

- 8 lean pork sausages
- 2 400g/14oz tins mixed beans, drained
- 2 400g/14oz tins chopped tomatoes
- 1 onion, chopped
- 2 carrots, chopped
- 1 tbsp tomato puree/paste or ketchup
- 1 tsp brown sugar
- 1 tsp Dijon/mild mustard
- Low cal cooking spray

1 Brown the sausages in the pan with the onions. Combine all the ingredients in the slow cooker and leave to cook for 3-4 hours on high or low for 5-6 hours with the lid tightly shut.

2 Check the sausages are properly cooked through and, if you want to thicken the sauce up, leave the lid off while you cook on high for up to 45 mins extra.

3 Serve on its own with crusty bread or with mashed potato and green veg.

Loved by kids and adults alike, this is a real cowboy's supper-time meal which always goes down a treat. It takes just minutes to put together and is a great way to get some vegetables into the kids.

AROMATIC KICKING PORK RIBS

SERVES 5 CALORIES PER SERVING 448

- 1kg/2¼ lbs pork ribs
- 1 tsp each garlic powder, chilli, cumin & basil
- ½ tsp salt
- 2 400g/14oz tins chopped tomatoes
- 1 tbsp ketchup
- 1 green chilli, chopped or a pinch of crushed chilli flakes to taste

1 Rub the dry spices onto the ribs. Add all the ingredients to the slow cooker and leave to cook with the lid tightly on for 5-6 hours on low.

2 Ensure the ribs are super tender and serve with rice and beans.

There are a number of different types of rib available depending on the cut from which they are taken. Choose whichever is cheapest or whichever you prefer. All will work well with this recipe.

SWEET & SOUR PINEAPPLE PORK

- SERVES 6
- CALORIES PER SERVING 238

- 900g/2lb lean cubed pork
- 1 tbsp plain/all purpose flour
- 1 400g/14oz tin pineapple chunks (reserve the juice)
- 1 onion, chopped
- 1 green (bell) pepper, chopped
- 2 carrots, cut into batons
- 1 tbsp brown sugar
- ½ tsp salt
- 2 tbsp lime juice
- 1 tbsp light soy sauce
- 120ml/½ cup vegetable stock
- Low cal cooking spray

1 Brown the pork in a frying pan with a little low cal spray. Remove from the pan and dust with the flour. Put all the other ingredients, except the pineapple chunks, into the slow cooker (include the pineapple juice).

2 Combine everything and leave to cook on low for 4-5 hours with the lid tightly closed.

3 Check the pork is tender and then add the pineapple chunks. Leave for a further 30 min and serve with boiled rice.

Sweet and sour is one of the most loved Chinese meals in the world. This is not supposed to be an authentic copy - just take it as a super simple replica which should satisfy your cravings.

SWEET SESAME SALMON KEBABS

- SERVES 4
- CALORIES PER SERVING 240

- 500g/1lb 2oz boneless salmon fillets, cubed
- 1 tbsp sesame oil
- 2 tbsp soy sauce
- 1 tbsp runny honey
- 2 garlic cloves, crushed
- ½ tsp ground ginger
- 8 skewers
- Salt & pepper to taste

1 Season and skewer the salmon pieces evenly.

2 Mix together the sesame oil, soy sauce, honey, garlic & ginger and brush onto the salmon kebabs (reserving any leftover sauce).

3 Cover and leave to cook on high for 1-2 hours or until the salmon is cooked through and tender.

4 Brush with a little more sauce or water during cooking if the salmon is drying out.

You could add some baby sweetcorn or button mushrooms to these kebabs if you like.

SUNNY HONEY DRUMSTICKS

SERVES 4 — CALORIES PER SERVING 210

- 8 skinless, chicken drumsticks
- 1 tbsp runny honey
- 1 tbsp rice wine vinegar
- 3 garlic cloves, crushed
- 60ml/¼ cup soy sauce
- 1 tsp paprika
- 1 red onion, sliced
- 2 tbsp freshly chopped parsley
- Low cal cooking oil spray
- Salt & pepper to taste

1 First pierce the drumsticks with a fork or skewer.

2 Mix together the honey, rice wine vinegar, garlic, soy sauce and paprika to make a marinade. Smother the drumsticks with this marinade and leave to chill for as long as you can (ideally overnight).

3 After this time, place the chicken and juices in the slow cooker with a little low cal spray. Cover and leave to cook on high for 2-3 hours or until the chicken is cooked through and piping hot.

4 Sprinkle with fresh parsley, season and serve as part of a lovely summer BBQ .

Piercing the chicken will encourage the marinade to penetrate deep into the meat.

BBQ SHREDDED BEEF

SERVES 4 — CALORIES PER SERVING 300

- 500g/1lb 2oz lean beef stewing steak, cubed
- 2 tbsp brown sugar
- 2 tbsp tomato puree/paste
- 2 onions, sliced
- 2 tbsp Dijon mustard
- 2 tbsp Worcestershire sauce
- 2 tbsp white wine vinegar
- 1 tsp paprika
- 3 garlic cloves crushed
- 120ml/½ cup tomato passata/paste
- Salt & pepper to taste

1 First place all the ingredients, except the stewing steak in a saucepan. Bring to the boil and reduce to a gentle simmer. Allow to cook for 8-10 minutes.

2 Place in a blender and blitz into a smooth BBQ sauce.

3 Check the seasoning and place the beef and BBQ sauce in the slow cooker. Cover and leave to cook on low for 8-10 hours or until the beef is meltingly tender (add a little water during cooking if you think the dish needs it).

4 Remove from the slow cooker and use 2 forks to shred. Check the seasoning and serve.

This shredded BBQ beef is a perfect low maintenance addition to a family BBQ that you can prepare ahead of time.

SLOW SCOTTISH STOVIES

SERVES 4 CALORIES PER SERVING 333

- 450g/1lb left over roast beef (or other cooked red meat)
- 175g/6oz potatoes, diced
- 2 large onions, chopped
- 250ml/1 cup vegetable stock
- Salt & pepper to taste

1 Combine all the ingredients together in the slow cooker and cook on low for 5-6 hours or high for 3-4 hours with the lid tightly shut. The liquid should all be gone by the end of the cooking time, if it hasn't, remove the lid and leave to cook for a little longer.

2 Stir through and serve in bowls with British brown sauce if you have it!

This is a great recipe to use up any cooked leftover red meat you might have. Traditionally it's served with plain Scottish oatcakes and it's super-simple to make. You can also used cubed corned beef in this recipe.

PEANUT BUTTER CHICKEN

SERVES 4 CALORIES PER SERVING 245

- 500g/1lb 2oz skinless chicken breast, diced
- 1 red (bell) pepper, sliced
- 1 onion, chopped
- 4 tbsp low fat peanut butter
- 2 tbsp lime juice
- 120ml/½ cup chicken stock
- 1 tbsp soy sauce
- 1 tsp each ground cumin & coriander
- ½ tsp paprika
- Salt & pepper to taste
- Low cal cooking spray

1 In a frying pan quickly brown the chicken in a little low cal spray.

2 Add all the ingredients to the slow cooker, season, cover and leave to cook on low for 4-5 hours or high for 3-4 hours. Make sure the chicken is cooked through and serve with noodles & beansprouts.

Peanut butter chicken is delicious. You can really 'lift' the dish by serving with fresh lime wedges.

ENCHILADA EL SALVADOR

SERVES 4 · CALORIES PER SERVING 324

- 450g/1lb lean, minced/ground beef
- 1 onion, chopped
- 1 green (bell) pepper, chopped
- 1 400g/14oz tin black beans, drained
- 2 400g/14oz tins chopped tomatoes
- 250ml/1 cup beef stock or boiling water
- ½ tsp chilli powder
- 4 tsp taco seasoning

Or make your own:

- 2 tsp mild chilli powder, 1 ½ tsp ground cumin, ½ tsp paprika, ¼ tsp each of onion powder, garlic powder, dried oregano & crushed chilli flakes, 1 tsp each of sea salt & black pepper

1 Add all the ingredients to the slow cooker and combine well. Leave to cook on low with the lid tightly on for 5-6 hours or 3-4 hours on high, until the beef is tender and cooked through. If you want to thicken it up a little leave, to cook for a further 45 mins with the lid off.

2 Serve with flour tortillas, shredded salad, grated cheese and sour cream (or Greek yoghurt).

Inspired by the flavours of Tex Mex this dish is great fun to eat as a family with everyone helping themselves across the table making their very own perfect enchilada!

CHICKEN & PINEAPPLE KEBABS

SERVES 4 · CALORIES PER SERVING 240

- 500g/1lb 2oz skinless free range chicken, cubed
- 200g/7oz drained tinned pineapple chunks (reserve the juice)
- 2 red peppers, cut into chunks
- 2 tsp dried oregano
- 1 tsp garlic powder
- 8 skewers
- Salt & pepper to taste

1 Season the chicken and place in a bowl with the reserved pineapple juice and red peppers; combine well.

2 Drain the juice from the bowl and sprinkle the chicken, pineapple & peppers with dried oregano & garlic powder.

3 Skewer the chicken, pineapple & pepper pieces in turn and place in the slow cooker. Cover and leave to cook on high for 3-4 hours or until chicken is cooked through and tender.

4 Check the seasoning and serve.

These light kebabs are delicious served with shredded salad and fat free Greek yoghurt for a perfect alfresco family meal.

RUSTIC CHICKEN STEW

SERVES 6 CALORIES PER SERVING 480

- 2kg/4½ lb skinless chicken pieces
- 2 tbsp plain/all purpose flour
- 1 onion, chopped
- 1 red (bell) pepper, sliced
- 2 cloves garlic, crushed
- 2 400g/14oz tins chopped tomatoes
- 1 tsp dried rosemary
- 1 handful pitted green olives
- 1 tsp anchovy paste
- 3 bay leaves
- 500ml/2 cups chicken stock
- Low cal cooking spray
- Salt & pepper to taste

1 Season the chicken pieces well. Dust with the flour and then quickly brown in a large pan with a little low cal cooking spray.

2 When browned, remove the chicken from the pan and place in the slow cooker with all the other ingredients. Leave to cook on low for 5-6 hours or high for 3-4 hours with the lid tightly shut or until the chicken is cooked through and tender.

3 If you prefer the sauce to be a little thicker, continue cooking for about 45 min on the high setting with the lid removed.

Widely known in Italy as 'Hunter's Stew', this hearty meal has kept the faith with countless hunters and gatherers over the years. Regional variations of this dish are common throughout Italy - this rustic version is one of the most popular.

BUDAPEST BEEF GOULASH

SERVES 6 CALORIES PER SERVING 228

- 900g/2lbs lean stewing beef cut into chunks (trim off any fat)
- 1 red (bell) pepper, sliced
- 3 cloves garlic, crushed
- 250ml/1 cup beef stock or water
- 250ml/1 cup red wine
- 1 400g/14oz tin chopped tomatoes
- 1 tbsp tomato puree/paste
- 1 tsp paprika
- 1½ tbsp plain/all purpose flour
- 1 onion, chopped
- Low cal cooking oil
- Salt & pepper to taste

1 Season the beef and quickly brown in a smoking hot pan with a little low cal spray. Remove from the pan and dust with flour (the easiest way is to put the beef and flour into a plastic bag and give it a good shake). Add all the ingredients to the slow cooker and combine well.

2 Leave to cook on low with the lid tightly shut for 5-6 hours or until the beef is tender and cooked through. If you want to thicken up a little, leave to cook for a further 45 mins with the lid off.

3 Lovely with a salad & some crusty bread or serve with sour cream and tagliatelle pasta.

Goulash is a European dish which suits the slow cooker beautifully. After hours of gentle cooking this 'tougher' meat becomes a tender cut which just melts in the mouth.

GINGER BEEF

SERVES 6 CALORIES PER SERVING 338

- 675g/1½lb silverside beef/round steak, cubed
- 2 garlic cloves, crushed
- 370ml/1½ cups beef stock
- 1 red (bell) pepper, sliced
- 4 carrots, sliced
- 1 onion, chopped
- 2 tbsp soy sauce
- 1 tbsp freshly grated ginger
- 1 tbsp cornflour mixed with 3 tbsp water
- 100g/3½oz frozen peas
- Salt & pepper to taste

1 Add all the ingredients, except the peas, to the slow cooker. Season well, cover and leave to cook on low for 5-6 hours or high for 3-4 hours.

2 An hour before the end of cooking, add the peas and continue to cook until both the beef and peas are tender.

Ginger and beef are a great combination and often used in Chinese cookery. Use low salt soy sauce if you want to be extra healthy.

ALMONDS, BEEF & OLIVES

SERVES 4 CALORIES PER SERVING 392

- 600g/1lb 5oz lean stewing steak cubed
- 250ml/1 cup beef stock
- 60ml/¼ cup red wine
- 200g/7oz pitted olives
- 1 tsp each smoked paprika, dried basil & rosemary
- 1 tbsp plain/all purpose flour
- 25g/1oz chopped almonds
- Salt & pepper to taste

1 Season the beef and coat well in the plain flour. Add all the ingredients, except the olives, to the slow cooker and leave to cook on low for 4-6 hours or until the beef is tender.

2 Add a little more stock or wine during cooking if needed and adjust the seasoning. 20 minutes before the end of cooking add the olives, warm through and serve.

This dish is delicious served with creamed spinach and/or honeyed carrots. Feel free to use a different mix of dried herbs to suit your taste. You can also add a tablespoon of tomato puree during cooking to thicken if you prefer.

LENTILS, SAUSAGES & PEAS

SERVES 4 • CALORIES PER SERVING 390

- 50g/2oz red lentils
- ½ tsp each crushed chilli flakes, ground cumin & coriander
- 1 onion, sliced
- 450g/1lb lean pork sausages
- 120ml/ ½ cup beef stock
- 150g/5oz frozen peas
- 1 tbsp Dijon mustard
- 2 tbsp freshly chopped flat leaf parsley
- Low cal cooking spray
- Salt & pepper to taste

1 Add a little low cal spray to a frying pan and quickly brown the sausages. Add all the ingredients to the slow cooker, stir well, cover and leave to cook on high for 2-3 hours or low for 4-5 hours. If you need more liquid during cooking add a little more stock.

2 Ensure the lentils are tender and the sausages cooked through. Serve with boiled potatoes and spinach.

You can serve the sausages whole or alternatively remove after cooking, slice in diagonals, return to the slow cooker and stir through before serving.

SPINACH & LAMB STEW

SERVES 4 • CALORIES PER SERVING 467

- 500g/1lb 2oz lean lamb cut into bite sized chunks (any lean cut will work)
- 2 cloves garlic, crushed
- Zest of 1 lemon
- 1 onion, chopped
- 2 400g/14oz tins chopped tomatoes
- 1 tbsp tomato puree/paste
- 1 400g/14oz tin chickpeas, drained
- 400g/14oz fresh spinach, chopped
- Salt & pepper to taste
- 2 tbsp low fat Greek yoghurt
- Low cal cooking spray

Dried herb mix of the following:

- 1 tsp each coriander & turmeric
- ½ tsp each ground cumin, black pepper & oregano

1 Gently sauté the onion in a little low cal oil, remove from the pan and then brown the lamb for a couple of minutes on a high heat.

2 Combine all ingredients together (except the yoghurt and spinach) in the slow cooker with the lid tightly shut and cook on low for 4-6 hours or until the lamb is tender and cooked through.

3 30mins before the end of cooking add the spinach, stir through the yoghurt before serving.

Super rich in iron & calcium, spinach is a super-food which is twinned beautifully in this dish with chickpeas, lemon zest and Greek-inspired spices.

MARRAKESH LAMB

SERVES 4 CALORIES PER SERVING 415

- 500g/1lb 2oz trimmed lamb cut into cubes (any lean cut will work)
- ½ tsp black pepper
- 1 tsp each ground cumin, coriander, ginger, turmeric, paprika & cinnamon
- 2 400g/14oz tins chopped tomatoes
- 75g/3oz red split lentils
- 1 lt/4 cups lamb stock or boiling water
- 2 onions, chopped
- 1 tsp brown sugar
- 5 cloves garlic, crushed

1 This one couldn't be any easier. No need to brown the meat, so just combine all the ingredients in the slow cooker, cover and leave to cook on low for 4-6 hours. Ensure the lamb is tender and cooked through. If you want to thicken up a little, leave to cook for a further 45 mins with the lid off.

2 Delicious served with low fat Greek yoghurt, couscous or fragrant rice.

Morocco's capital is world renowned for its tagine cuisine. Slow cookers provide a wonderful alternative to this specialist style of cooking. This recipe is a lovely North African-inspired dish which, if its new to you, should piqué your interest in Moroccan cooking.

APRICOT & PORK CASSEROLE

SERVES 4 CALORIES PER SERVING 275

- 2 yellow or orange peppers, sliced
- 2 onions, sliced
- 1 garlic clove, crushed
- 500g/1lb 2oz pork tenderloin, cut into 2cm thick slices
- 125g/4oz dried apricots, chopped
- 1 tsp brown sugar
- 200g/7oz ripe plum tomatoes, chopped
- 2 tbsp tomato puree
- Low cal cooking oil spray
- Salt & pepper to taste

1 Gently sauté the peppers, onions & garlic in a little low cal spray until softened.

2 Add the sautéed vegetables to the slow cooker along with all the other ingredients.

3 Gently combine, cover and leave to cook on low for 3-5 hours or until the pork is tender and cooked through.

4 Season and serve.

This dish is great served with salad, flat bread or couscous.

MUSHROOM CHILLI STEAK CASSEROLE

SERVES 4 CALORIES PER SERVING 300

- 2 red peppers, thinly sliced
- 2 onions, sliced
- 2 garlic cloves, finely sliced
- 4 large portabella mushrooms
- 500g/1lb 2oz lean beef stewing steak
- 2 tbsp soy sauce
- 2 tbsp Worcestershire sauce
- 60ml/¼ cup beef stock
- 1 bunch spring onions, sliced lengthways into ribbons
- Low cal cooking oil spray
- Salt & pepper to taste

1 Gently sauté the peppers, onions, garlic & mushrooms in a little low cal spray until softened.

2 Add the sautéed vegetables to the slow cooker along with all the other ingredients, except the spring onions.

3 Gently combine, cover and leave to cook on low for 7-9 hours or until the beef is meltingly tender (add a little more stock during cooking if needed).

4 Season and serve with the sliced spring onions on top.

Large flat Portabella mushrooms are available all year round but they are at their best in the spring.

MARMALADE CHICKEN CASSEROLE

SERVES 4 CALORIES PER SERVING 390

- 500g/1lb 2oz skinless chicken breasts
- 1 tbsp plain/all purpose flour
- 2 garlic cloves, crushed
- 2 tbsp orange marmalade
- 60ml/¼ cup fresh orange juice
- 60ml/¼ cup chicken stock
- 2 tbsp tomato puree/paste
- ½ tsp each brown sugar & salt
- 200g/7oz long grain rice
- 1 bunch spring onions, sliced lengthways into ribbons
- Low cal cooking oil spray
- Salt & pepper to taste

1 First, dust the chicken breast with flour until well covered and place in the slow cooker.

2 Mix together the garlic, marmalade, orange juice, stock, puree, salt & sugar and add to the slow cooker covering the dusted chicken as much as possible. Cover and leave to cook on low for 4-5 hours or until the chicken is cooked through.

3 Meanwhile cook the rice in salted boiling water until tender.

4 Season and serve with the sliced spring onions and any juices drizzled over the top on a bed of boiled rice.

This is a light, sweet, summer supper, which the whole family will enjoy.

FRESH GINGER CASHEW CHICKEN

- SERVES 4
- CALORIES PER SERVING 400

- 500g/1lb 2oz skinless chicken breasts, cubed
- 1 tbsp plain/all purpose flour
- 2 tbsp freshly grated ginger
- 2 garlic cloves, crushed
- 60ml/¼ chicken stock
- 1 tbsp tomato puree/paste
- ½ tsp each brown sugar, crushed chilli flakes & salt
- 100g/3½oz cashew nuts
- 200g/7oz egg noodles
- Low cal cooking oil spray
- Salt & pepper to taste

1 First dust the cubed chicken with flour until well covered.

2 Quickly brown the chicken in a frying pan with a little low cal oil.

3 Place in the slow cooker with all the other ingredients, except the nuts & noodles. Cover and leave to cook on low for 3-4 hours or until the chicken is cooked through.

4 Meanwhile cook the noodles in salted boiling water until tender.

5 Toss the chicken, juices and noodles together and sprinkle the cashew nuts over the top. Season & serve.

Adding the cashew nuts as a garnish gives this dish a crunch. You can add them during cooking if your prefer.

WHITE BEAN & LEEK CHICKEN STEW

- SERVES 4
- CALORIES PER SERVING 480

- 2 leeks, chopped
- 2 garlic cloves, crushed
- 500g/1lb 2oz skinless chicken breasts, cubed
- 60ml/¼ chicken stock
- 2 tsp dried rosemary
- 400g/14oz tinned white beans, drained
- 200g/7oz egg noodles
- Lime wedges to serve
- 1 avocado, diced
- Low cal cooking oil spray
- Salt & pepper to taste

1 Gently sauté the leeks & garlic in a little low cal oil for a few minutes until softened.

2 Place in the slow cooker with all the other ingredients, except the noodles, lime wedges & avocado. Cover and leave to cook on low for 3-4 hours or until the chicken is cooked through.

3 Meanwhile cook the noodles in salted boiling water until tender.

4 Toss the chicken stew and noodles together.

5 Serve with the lime wedges on the side & diced avocado arranged over the top.

Adding the avocado & lime wedges give this dish a really fresh feel.

BASIL & PARMESAN CHICKEN STEW

SERVES 4 CALORIES PER SERVING 230

- 2 onions, sliced
- 2 garlic cloves, crushed
- 500g/1lb 2oz skinless chicken breasts, cubed
- 60ml/¼ cup chicken stock
- 400g/14oz fresh ripe plum tomatoes
- 200g/7oz baby courgettes, sliced lengthways
- 50g/2oz Parmesan cheese
- 1 large bunch fresh basil, roughly chopped
- Low cal cooking oil spray
- Salt & pepper to taste

1 Gently sauté the onion & garlic in a little low cal oil for a few minutes until softened.

2 Place in the slow cooker with all the other ingredients, except the Parmesan cheese. (Reserve a little fresh basil for garnish).

3 Cover and leave to cook on low for 3-4 hours or until the chicken is cooked through. Season and serve.

Feel free to use tinned tomatoes if you don't have fresh tomatoes to hand.

CHINESE BEEF & PAK CHOI CASSEROLE

SERVES 4 CALORIES PER SERVING 325

- 500g/1lb 2oz lean beef stewing steak, cubed
- 1 tbsp plain/all purpose flour
- 1 tsp Chinese 5 spice powder
- 2 onions, sliced
- 4 garlic cloves, crushed
- 1 red chilli, finely chopped
- 250ml/1 cup beef stock
- 3 pak choi sliced lengthways
- 3 tbsp soy sauce
- 1 tsp brown sugar
- Low cal cooking oil spray
- Salt & pepper to taste

1 First toss the steak, flour and Chinese 5 spice together to cover the meat.

2 Quickly brown in a frying pan with a little low cal spray and set to one side.

3 Use the same pan to gently sauté the onions, garlic & chilli and then place everything in the slow cooker.

4 Cover and leave to cook on low for 6-8 hours or until the beef is really tender (add a little more stock if needed during cooking).

5 Season and serve.

Pak choi is a popular Chinese cabbage also known as bok choi. If you want it to retain some fresh crunch, hold off placing in the slow cooker until half an hour before the end of cooking.

CELERIAC & ORANGE BEEF STEW

SERVES 4 · CALORIES PER SERVING 320

- 2 leeks, sliced
- 3 garlic cloves, crushed
- 500g/1lb 2oz lean beef stewing steak, cubed
- 750g/1lb 11oz celeriac, diced
- 250ml/1 cup beef stock
- 60ml/ ¼ cup dry white wine
- Juice and zest of 1 large orange
- 3 tbsp soy sauce
- 200g/7oz baby sweetcorn, chopped
- Low cal cooking oil spray
- Salt & pepper to taste

1 Gently sauté the leeks & garlic until softened.

2 Place everything in the slow cooker, except the baby sweetcorn, Cover and leave to cook on low for 6-8 hours or until the beef is really tender.

3 20 minutes before the end of cooking add the baby sweetcorn.

4 Season and serve.

Beef stews can be quite heavy but this light stew is lifted by the citrus of the orange.

CITRUS CHICKEN

SERVES 4 · CALORIES PER SERVING 200

- 500g/1lb 2oz skinless chicken breasts
- 3 tbsp lime juice
- Bunch fresh coriander chopped and some to garnish
- 1 sliced green chilli (or a pinch of dried chilli flakes)
- 400g/14oz salsa (or make your own)

Salsa: Add 1 onion chopped, 1 clove garlic crushed, 1 green chilli chopped to 2 x 400g/14oz tins chopped tomatoes + sea salt to taste

- 4 tsp taco seasoning (or make your own)

Taco Seasoning: 2 tsp mild chilli powder, 1 ½ tsp ground cumin, ½ tsp paprika, ¼ tsp each of onion powder, garlic powder, dried oregano & crushed chilli flakes, 1 tsp each of sea salt & black pepper

1 Put everything together in the slow cooker making sure the chicken is covered with the rest of the ingredients. With the lid tightly shut, leave to cook for 4-5 hours on high or 5-6 hours on the low setting.

2 Ensure the chicken is cooked through and tender then shred it a little with 2 forks and serve with a fresh green salad/rice or quesadillas (flour tortilla).

Packed with protein, skinless chicken breasts are a great low fat meat to use in the slow cooker. The citrus lightness of this recipe is perfect. for summer months as well as a welcome taste bud infusion during the colder seasons.

PANCETTA RISOTTO

SERVES 4 — CALORIES PER SERVING 340

- 75g/3oz pancetta bacon, trimmed & diced
- 1 onion, sliced
- 1 garlic clove, crushed
- 300g/11oz Arborio risotto rice
- 1lt/4 cups chicken stock
- 200g/7oz rocket
- Low cal cooking oil spray
- Salt & pepper to taste

1 First sauté the pancetta, onion & garlic in a little low cal oil for a few minutes.

2 Remove from the pan and chop as finely as possible. Return to the pan and add the rice. Stir around well to coat the rice in the residual oil.

3 Place the contents of the pan in the slow cooker along with the stock. Combine well, cover and leave to cook on low for approx 2 hours or until the stock has been absorbed.

4 Check the rice; if it is not tender add some more stock and leave to cook for a little longer.

5 When the risotto is tender and the stock has been absorbed, season and serve with the rocket.

Chopping the sautéed pancetta and onions as small as possible means their lovely salty-sweet flavour will permeate every mouthful of this lovely risotto.

SPRING PEA & PARMESAN RISOTTO

SERVES 4 — CALORIES PER SERVING 380

- 1 onion, sliced
- 2 garlic cloves, crushed
- 300g/11oz Arborio risotto rice
- 1lt/4 cups chicken or vegetable stock
- 300g/7oz fresh peas
- 25g/1oz Parmesan cheese shavings
- 1 tbsp olive oil
- Salt & pepper to taste

1 First sauté the onion & garlic in the olive oil for a few minutes.

2 Add the rice to the pan and stir well to coat each grain in the olive oil.

3 Place the contents of the pan in the slow cooker along with the stock and peas. Combine well, cover and leave to cook on low for approx 2 hours or until the stock has been absorbed.

4 Check the rice; if it is not tender add some more stock and leave to cook for a little longer.

5 When the risotto is tender and the stock has been absorbed, season and serve with the Parmesan shavings on top.

Frozen peas will work just as nicely as fresh peas. If you are using fresh peas you may wish hold off adding them to the slow cooker until 30 minutes before the end of cooking so that they retain some 'crunch'.

TOMATO & FRESH BASIL RISOTTO

SERVES 4 CALORIES PER SERVING 345

- 1 onion, sliced
- 2 garlic cloves, crushed
- 1 tbsp olive oil
- 300g/11oz Arborio risotto rice
- 400g/14oz fresh chopped tomatoes
- 500ml/2 cups chicken or vegetable stock
- 125g/4oz rocket
- 4 tbsp freshly chopped basil
- Salt & pepper to taste

1 First sauté the onion & garlic in the olive oil for a few minutes.

2 Add the rice to the pan and stir well to coat each grain in the olive oil.

3 Place the contents of the pan in the slow cooker along with the chopped tomatoes & stock. Combine well, cover and leave to cook on low for approx 2 hours or until all the liquid has been absorbed.

4 Check the rice; if it is not tender add some more stock and leave to cook for a little longer.

5 When the risotto is tender and the stock has been absorbed, season and serve with the chopped basil on top and the rocket on the side.

You could also add a little sundried tomato paste to this dish to give additional depth.

SQUASH & GOATS CHEESE RISOTTO

SERVES 4 CALORIES PER SERVING 370

- 1 large butternut squash, peeled, deseeded & sliced into matchsticks
- 1 onion, sliced
- 2 garlic cloves, crushed
- 1 tbsp olive oil
- 300g/11oz Arborio risotto rice
- 1lt/4 cups chicken or vegetable stock
- 50g/2oz goat's cheese, crumbled
- Salt & pepper to taste

1 First sauté the squash, onion & garlic in the olive oil for a few minutes (ensure you cut the squash finely otherwise you will find the rice is tender before the squash is ready).

2 Add the rice to the pan and stir well to coat each grain in the olive oil.

3 Place the contents of the pan in the slow cooker along with the stock. Combine well, cover and leave to cook on low for approx 2 hours or until all the liquid has been absorbed.

4 Check the rice; if it is not tender add some more stock and leave to cook for a little longer.

5 When the risotto is tender and the stock has been absorbed, season and serve with the goat's cheese crumbled over the top.

Add a little dried sage to the slow cooker if you have it or garnish with fresh sage leaves if you like.

 For side dishes see page 7

THAI BEEF CURRY

SERVES 4 CALORIES PER SERVING 330

- 500g/1lb 2oz lean sirloin steak, thickly sliced
- 2 tbsp Thai green curry paste
- 1 red onion, sliced
- 2 garlic cloves, crushed
- 1 red pepper, sliced
- 2 tsp dried basil
- 1 tbsp each Thai fish sauce, lime juice & soy sauce
- 250ml/1 cup beef stock
- 150g/5oz trimmed green beans
- 1 tbsp coconut cream
- Salt & pepper to taste
- Low cal cooking oil spray

1 Season the steak and quickly brown for a couple of minutes in a frying pan with a little low cal oil.

2 Remove from the heat and place in the slow cooker along with all the other ingredients except the coconut cream.

3 Combine well, cover and leave to cook on high for 3-5 hours or until the steak is tender and cooked through.

4 Add the coconut cream to the slow cooker. Gently stir through and serve.

You could substitute sugar snap peas or mange tout for green beans in this dish if you prefer.

LAMB JALFREZI

SERVES 4 CALORIES PER SERVING 310

- 500g/1lb 2oz lean lamb fillet, cubed
- 1 onion, finely chopped
- 2 garlic cloves, crushed
- 4 green chillies, finely sliced lengthways
- 400g/14oz tinned chopped tomatoes
- 2 tbsp tomato puree/paste
- 60ml/¼ cup vegetable stock
- ½ tsp each cumin, turmeric, paprika, garam masala, ground coriander, ginger, cayenne pepper, brown sugar & salt
- Salt & pepper to taste
- Low cal cooking oil spray

1 Season the lamb and quickly brown for a couple of minutes in a frying pan with a little low cal oil.

2 Remove from the heat and place in the slow cooker along with all the other ingredients.

3 Combine well, cover and leave to cook on low for 5-7 hours or until the lamb is tender and cooked through.

Jalfrezi is a very popular dish, which traditionally contains fresh green chillies.

BEEF MADRAS

SERVES 4 CALORIES PER SERVING 310

- 500g/1lb 2oz lean beef stewing steak, cubed
- 2 onions, sliced
- 2 garlic cloves, crushed
- 1 tbsp hot curry powder
- ½ tsp each cumin, turmeric, ground coriander, brown sugar & salt
- 3 tbsp tomato puree/paste
- 400g/14oz tinned chopped tomatoes
- 60ml/¼ cup beef stock
- 2 tsp lemon juice
- Salt & pepper to taste
- Low cal cooking oil spray

1 Season the beef and quickly brown for a couple of minutes in a frying pan with a little low cal oil.

2 Remove from the heat and place in the slow cooker along with all the other ingredients.

3 Combine well, cover and leave to cook on low for 5-7 hours or until the beef is tender and cooked through.

Madras is a hot curry. Feel free to alter the spice to suit your own palate.

ROGAN JOSH

SERVES 4 CALORIES PER SERVING 290

- 500g/1lb 2oz skinless chicken breast meat, cubed
- 4 onions, sliced
- 2 garlic cloves, crushed
- 400g/14oz tinned chopped tomatoes
- 1 tsp turmeric
- 3 tbsp tomato puree/paste
- 60ml/¼ cup chicken stock
- ½ tsp each garam masala, ground coriander, cumin, paprika, hot chilli powder, ground ginger & salt
- 200g/7oz potatoes, finely chopped
- 1 tsp brown sugar
- Salt & pepper to taste
- Low cal cooking oil spray

1 Season the chicken and quickly brown for a couple of minutes in a frying pan with a little low cal oil.

2 Remove from the heat and place in the slow cooker along with all the other ingredients.

3 Combine well, cover and leave to cook on high for 4-6 hours or until the chicken is tender and cooked through.

This curry should have a thick onion and tomato base. Leave to cook for a little longer if it needs thickening.

CHICKEN KEEMA

SERVES 4 CALORIES PER SERVING 280

- 500g/1lb 2oz lean chicken or turkey mince
- 2 onions, sliced
- 2 garlic cloves, crushed
- ½ tsp each turmeric, ground cumin & coriander
- 2 tsp hot curry powder
- 200g/7oz peas
- 2 tbsp tomato puree/paste
- 180ml/¾ cup chicken stock
- 120ml/½ fat free Greek yoghurt
- Salt & pepper to taste
- Low cal cooking oil spray

1 Season the mince and quickly brown for a couple of minutes in a frying pan with a little low cal oil.

2 Remove from the heat and place in the slow cooker along with all the other ingredients except the yoghurt.

3 Combine well, cover and leave to cook on high for 3-5 hours or until the mince is cooked through.

4 Add the Greek yoghurt to the slow cooker. Gently stir through and serve.

Frozen peas are fine to use for this recipe. Place them in a little boiling water for a minute or two to warm through before adding to the slow cooker.

'BUTTER' CHICKEN

SERVES 4 CALORIES PER SERVING 270

- 500g/1lb 2oz skinless chicken breast meat, cubed
- 2 tbsp low fat olive spread
- 2 garlic cloves, crushed
- ½ tsp each ground turmeric, cumin, coriander, paprika, ginger, crushed chilli flakes, garam masala & salt
- 1 tsp brown sugar
- 250ml/1 cup tomato passata/sieved tomatoes
- 60ml/¼ cup vegetable stock
- 3 tbsp tomato puree/paste
- 120ml/½ cup fat free Greek yoghurt
- Salt & pepper to taste
- Low cal cooking oil spray

1 Season the chicken and seal for a couple of minutes in a frying pan with a little low cal oil.

2 Remove from the heat and place in the slow cooker along with all the other ingredients except the yoghurt.

3 Combine well, cover and leave to cook on high for 3-5 hours or until the chicken is tender and cooked through.

4 Add the yoghurt to the slow cooker. Gently stir through and serve.

This is a great 'skinny' version of the classic calorific dish.

CHICKEN BHUNA

SERVES 4 CALORIES PER SERVING 230

- 500g/1lb 2oz skinless chicken breast meat, cubed
- 1 onion, finely chopped
- 60ml/ ¼ cup chicken stock
- 250g/9oz mixture of chopped carrots, cauliflower & peas
- 2 garlic cloves, crushed
- 2 tbsp tomato puree/paste
- 400g/14oz tinned chopped tomatoes
- ½ tsp each cumin, turmeric, paprika, garam masala, medium chilli powder, ground coriander, brown sugar & salt
- A pinch of cardamom and fenugreek seeds
- 1 tbsp fat free Greek yoghurt
- Salt & pepper to taste
- Low cal cooking oil spray

1 Season the chicken and quickly brown for a couple of minutes in a frying pan with a little low cal oil.

2 Remove from the heat and place in the slow cooker along with all the other ingredients except the Greek yoghurt.

3 Combine well, cover and leave to cook on high for 3-5 hours or until the chicken is tender and cooked through.

4 Add the yoghurt to the slow cooker. Gently stir through and serve.

Use any mixture of vegetables you prefer for this classic medium dish.

CHICKEN DOPIAZA

SERVES 4 CALORIES PER SERVING 260

- 500g/1lb 2oz skinless chicken breast meat, cubed
- 4 onions, thickly sliced
- 2 garlic cloves, crushed
- ½ tsp each cumin, turmeric, paprika, garam masala, hot chilli powder, ground coriander, ginger, brown sugar & salt
- 2 tbsp tomato puree/paste
- 180/¾ cup tomato passata/sieved tomatoes
- 60ml/¼ cup chicken stock
- Salt & pepper to taste
- Low cal cooking oil spray

1 Season the chicken and quickly brown for a couple of minutes in a frying pan with a little low cal oil.

2 Remove from the heat and place in the slow cooker along with all the other ingredients.

3 Combine well, cover and leave to cook on high for 3-5 hours or until the chicken is tender and cooked through.

Onions and a thick sauce are the calling cards of this curry.

 For side dishes see page 7

GARLIC CHICKEN

SERVES 4 CALORIES PER SERVING 240

- 500g/1lb 2oz skinless chicken breast meat, cubed
- 14 garlic cloves, peeled & finely sliced
- 1 onion, chopped
- ½ tsp each cumin, turmeric, paprika, garam masala, hot chilli powder, ground coriander, brown sugar & salt
- 1 tbsp tomato puree/paste
- 2 vine ripened tomatoes, roughly chopped
- 180ml/¾ cup tomato passata/sieved tomatoes
- 60ml/¼ cup chicken stock
- Salt & pepper to taste
- Low cal cooking oil spray

1 Season the chicken and gently sauté for a couple of minutes in a frying pan with a little low cal oil and the sliced garlic.

2 Remove from the heat and place in the slow cooker along with all the other ingredients.

3 Combine well, cover and leave to cook on high for 3-5 hours or until the chicken is tender and cooked through.

Be careful not to burn the garlic when you sauté with the chicken. A few drops of water in the pan can help prevent this.

CHICKEN KORMA

SERVES 4 CALORIES PER SERVING 260

- 500g/1lb 2oz skinless chicken breast meat, cubed
- 2 garlic cloves, crushed
- 1 onion, chopped
- 2 tsp mild curry powder
- ½ tsp each cumin, turmeric, paprika & salt
- 2 tbsp tomato puree/paste
- 250ml/1 cup tomato passata/sieved tomatoes
- 60ml/¼ cup low fat coconut milk
- 1 tbsp ground almonds
- Salt & pepper to taste
- Low cal cooking oil spray

1 Season the chicken and quickly brown for a couple of minutes in a frying pan with a little low cal oil.

2 Remove from the heat and place in the slow cooker along with all the other ingredients except the coconut milk & ground almonds.

3 Combine well, cover and leave to cook on high for 3-5 hours or until the chicken is tender and cooked through.

4 Add the coconut milk to the slow cooker. Gently stir through and serve with the ground almonds sprinkled over the top.

Korma dishes are traditionally 'nutty'. This version contains both coconut milk and ground almonds.

TANDOORI CHICKEN

SERVES 4 · CALORIES PER SERVING 370

- 12 chicken drumsticks
- Juice and zest from 1 lemon
- 2 garlic cloves, crushed
- 1 tbsp tomato puree/paste
- 1 tsp mild chilli powder
- ½ tsp each salt, cumin, turmeric, paprika & black pepper
- 250ml/1 cup fat free Greek yoghurt
- Salt & pepper to taste
- Low cal cooking oil spray

1 Mix together all the ingredients, except the chicken, to form a yoghurt paste.

2 Season the chicken and smother with the yoghurt paste.

3 Place in the slow cooker, cover and leave to cook on high for 2-4 hours or until the chicken is tender and cooked through.

This dish is great served with a simple green salad.

EGG CURRY

SERVES 4 · CALORIES PER SERVING 260

- 8 hardboiled peeled eggs, halved
- 2 garlic cloves, crushed
- 2 onions, chopped
- 2 tsp mild curry powder
- ½ tsp each cumin, turmeric, paprika & salt
- 2 tbsp tomato puree/paste
- 250ml/1 cup tomato passata/sieved tomatoes
- 12oml/½ cup low fat coconut milk
- Salt & pepper to taste
- Low cal cooking oil spray

1 Place all the ingredients in the slow cooker, except the coconut milk and eggs.

2 Combine well, cover and leave to cook on high for 2 hours.

3 Add the boiled eggs and leave to warm through for 30-40 mins.

4 Add the coconut milk, combine well and serve.

Egg curries are a very popular main course in India. Use organic eggs for the best yolks.

CHICKEN DHANSAK

SERVES 4 • CALORIES PER SERVING 270

- 500g/1lb 2oz skinless chicken breast meat, cubed
- 2 onions, chopped
- 2 garlic cloves, crushed
- ½ tsp each cumin, turmeric, paprika, garam masala, ground coriander, ginger, brown sugar & salt
- 2 tbsp tomato puree/paste
- 250ml/1 cup tomato passata/sieved tomatoes
- 60ml/ ¼ cup chicken stock
- 125g/4oz pineapple chunks, chopped
- Salt & pepper to taste
- Low cal cooking oil spray

1 Season the chicken and quickly brown for a couple of minutes in a frying pan with a little low cal oil.

2 Remove from the heat and place in the slow cooker along with all the other ingredients except the pineapple chunks.

3 Combine well, cover and leave to cook on high for 3-5 hours or until the chicken is tender and cooked through.

4 45 minutes before the end of cooking add the pineapple chunks to the slow cooker.

5 Season and serve.

You could also use fresh pineapple for this dish if you prefer.

CHICKEN PASANDA

SERVES 4 • CALORIES PER SERVING 300

- 500g/1lb 2oz skinless chicken breast meat, cubed
- 2 garlic cloves, crushed
- 1 onion, chopped
- 1 tbsp mild curry powder
- ½ tsp salt & brown sugar
- 3 tbsp tomato puree/paste
- 250ml/1 cup tomato passata/sieved tomatoes
- 60ml/¼ cup chicken stock
- 60ml/¼ cup fat free Greek yoghurt
- 2 tbsp chopped cashew nuts
- Salt & pepper to taste
- Low cal cooking oil spray

1 Season the chicken and quickly brown for a couple of minutes in a frying pan with a little low cal oil.

2 Remove from the heat and place in the slow cooker along with all the other ingredients except the yoghurt & cashew nuts. Combine well, cover and leave to cook on high for 3-5 hours or until the chicken is tender and cooked through.

3 Meanwhile gently toast the chopped cashew nuts in the frying pan with a little low cal oil for 2-3 minutes until they begin to brown and become fragrant.

4 When the chicken is ready add the Greek yoghurt to the slow cooker. Gently stir through and serve with the toasted cashew nuts sprinkled over the top.

Toasted almonds also work well for this dish in place of cashew nuts.

CORIANDER & SWEET POTATO CURRY

SERVES 4 · CALORIES PER SERVING 160

- 500g/1lb 2oz sweet potatoes, cubed
- 2 onions, finely chopped
- ½ tsp each turmeric, mild chilli powder, cumin, coriander, paprika & salt
- 1 red chilli, finely chopped
- 2 carrots, sliced into batons
- 120ml/½ cup vegetable stock
- 120ml/½ cup low fat coconut milk
- 2 tbsp freshly chopped coriander
- Lime wedges to serve
- Salt & pepper to taste
- Low cal cooking oil spray

1 Place all the ingredients in the slow cooker, except the coconut milk, chopped coriander & lime wedges.

2 Combine well, cover and leave to cook on high for 3-5 hours or until the vegetables are tender and cooked through.

3 Add the coconut milk to the slow cooker. Gently stir through, sprinkle with chopped coriander and serve with the lime wedges.

Sweet potatoes are a fantastic versatile vegetable, which form the base of many Caribbean curries.

ALOO GOBI

SERVES 4 · CALORIES PER SERVING 160

- 1 large cauliflower head, split into florets
- ½ green cabbage, shredded
- 200g/7oz potatoes, cubed
- 400g/14oz tinned chopped tomatoes
- 2 garlic cloves, crushed
- 1 onion, chopped
- 1 tsp turmeric
- ½ tsp each cayenne pepper, cumin, coriander, paprika, garam masala, salt & brown sugar
- 2 tbsp tomato puree/paste
- 60ml/¼ cup vegetable stock
- 2 tbsp chopped coriander
- Salt & pepper to taste
- Low cal cooking oil spray

1 Place all the ingredients in the slow cooker, except the chopped coriander.

2 Combine well, cover and leave to cook on high for 3-5 hours or until the vegetables are tender and cooked through.

3 Sprinkle with chopped coriander and serve.

Spinach and broccoli make good additions to this dish too.

 For side dishes see page 7

SIMPLE VEGETABLE CURRY

SERVES 4 CALORIES PER SERVING 170

- 2 carrots cut into batons
- 1 large cauliflower head, split into florets
- 200g/7oz spinach leaves
- 125g/4oz peas
- 2 onions, chopped
- 400g/14oz tinned chopped tomatoes
- 2 garlic cloves, crushed
- 1 tbsp mild curry powder
- ½ tsp each salt & brown sugar
- 2 tbsp tomato puree/paste
- 60ml/¼ cup vegetable stock
- Salt & pepper to taste
- Low cal cooking oil spray

1 Place all the ingredients in the slow cooker.

2 Combine well, cover and leave to cook on high for 3-5 hours or until the vegetables are tender and cooked through.

Try adding some fresh sliced chillies as a garnish.

SAAG ALOO

SERVES 4 CALORIES PER SERVING 160

- 400g/14oz spinach leaves
- ½ green cabbage, shredded
- 200g/7oz potatoes, cubed
- 2 garlic cloves, crushed
- 1 onion, chopped
- 120ml/ ½ cup vegetable stock
- ½ tsp each turmeric, ginger, cumin, coriander, paprika & mustard seeds
- 2 tbsp freshly chopped coriander
- Lemon wedges to serve
- Salt & pepper to taste
- Low cal cooking oil spray

1 Place all the ingredients in the slow cooker, except the chopped coriander & lemon wedges.

2 Combine well, cover and leave to cook on high for 3-5 hours or until the vegetables are tender and cooked through.

3 Sprinkle with chopped coriander, place the lemon wedges on the side and serve.

If you have time, you could first quickly sauté the mustard seeds in a little low cal oil for a minute or two until they begin to pop.

PINEAPPLE & PRAWN CURRY

- SERVES 4
- CALORIES PER SERVING 210

- 500g/1lb 2oz raw, shelled king prawns
- ½ tsp each turmeric, brown sugar & salt
- 1 tbsp medium curry powder
- 2 tsp each fish sauce & tamarind paste
- 200g/7oz tinned pineapple, chopped
- 1 lemongrass stalk, finely chopped
- 2 garlic cloves, crushed
- 1 onion, chopped
- 2 tbsp tomato puree/paste
- 120ml/½ cup low fat coconut milk
- Salt & pepper to taste
- Low cal cooking oil spray

1 Place all the ingredients in the slow cooker.

2 Combine well, cover and leave to cook on high for 1-3 hours or until the prawns are cooked through.

The pineapple and tamarind combine well to give a lovely sweet & sour taste.

THAI FISH CURRY

- SERVES 4
- CALORIES PER SERVING 270

- 500g/1lb 2oz firm white fish fillets, cubed
- 2 garlic cloves, crushed
- ½ red chilli, finely chopped
- 2 onions, sliced
- Zest and juice of ½ lime
- 3 tbsp Thai green curry paste
- ½ tsp ground coriander
- 12oml/½ cup chicken stock
- 60ml/¼ cup low fat coconut milk
- Salt & pepper to taste
- Low cal cooking oil spray

1 Place all the ingredients in the slow cooker, except the coconut milk.

2 Combine well, cover and leave to cook on high for 1-3 hours or until the fish is cooked through.

3 Add the coconut milk and combine well.

Any type of firm white fish will work for this dish. Ensure the bones and skin are removed.

GREEN THAI FISH CURRY

SERVES 4 — CALORIES PER SERVING 215

- 500g/1lb 2oz meaty white fish fillets (go for whatever is on sale) haddock, cod, Pollock or cobbler
- 3 onions, chopped
- 1 tsp fresh ginger or ½ tsp ground ginger
- 3 cloves garlic, crushed
- 150g/5oz green beans
- 1 red chilli, chopped
- 50g/2oz watercress
- 2 tbsp Thai green curry paste
- 500ml/2 cups low fat coconut milk
- Low cal cooking spray
- Salt & pepper to taste

1 Sauté the onions & green beans with the ginger and garlic over a low heat in a little low cal spray. Season the fish fillets and carefully combine all the ingredients (except the watercress) in the slow cooker. Cook on low for 1 ½ hours with the lid tightly shut. This timing should mean your fish is not overcooked and the green beans have some bite to them.

2 Check the fish is properly cooked through by flaking it a little with a fork and gently add the watercress salad to the mix before serving. Serve with noodles or rice.

3 If you want to make it a little spicier you could add some more chopped chilli or crushed chilli flakes.

Compared to meat, fish cooks more quickly in the slow cooker and as such fish recipes can be really handy if you're pushed for time. .This recipe is a fantastic and easy Thai curry which is simple to prepare and doesn't take long at all in the slow cooker.

SWEET & CITRUS SALMON

SERVES 4 — CALORIES PER SERVING 270

- 500g/1lb 2oz thick boneless salmon fillets
- 1 onion, chopped
- 1 tbsp light soy sauce
- Juice of 1 fresh lime or 3 tbsp Lime juice
- 2 garlic cloves, crushed
- 1 tsp sugar dissolved into 3 tbsp warm water and brushed onto the fillets
- Low cal cooking spray
- Salt & pepper to taste

1 Chop the onion and sauté for a couple of minutes with the garlic in a little low cal oil. Remove from the pan and carefully combine all the ingredients in the slow cooker. Cook on low for 1½ hours with the lid tightly on.

2 Check the fish is properly cooked by flaking it a little with a fork and serve with salad potatoes and carrots. Alternatively, use in a lovely warm salad served with a little crusty bread.

Salmon can be relatively expensive so you can substitute for tilapia or basa or talk to your fishmonger for recommendations.

TUNA & NOODLE CATTIA

SERVES 4 CALORIES PER SERVING 250

- 350g/12oz fresh egg noodles
- 1 onion, chopped
- 1 400g/14oz tin fat free condensed mushroom soup
- 2 200g/7oz tins tuna steaks or flakes in water
- 100g/3½ oz frozen peas
- 1 tsp garlic powder
- Salt & pepper to taste
- Pinch of crushed chilli flakes

1 Quickly cook the noodles in salted boiling water. Save 3 tbsp of the drained water and then combine all the ingredients and saved water in the slow cooker. Cover and leave to cook on low for 1½ hours.

2 This is great served with a sliced red onion & tomato salad and a little parmesan.

An absolute classic American slow cooker recipe, Tuna & Noodle casserole is always a winner. This version takes it back to basics using the simplest store cupboard ingredients. The title 'Cattia' pays homage to the ancient Latin roots where the word 'casserole' has its origins.

CORIANDER & GARLIC PRAWNS

SERVES 4 CALORIES PER SERVING 269

- 500g/1lb 2oz raw king prawns
- 200g/7oz frozen peas
- 1 tsp sunflower oil
- 2 onions, sliced
- 200g/8oz cherry tomatoes, halved
- 1 tsp ground ginger
- 4 garlic cloves, crushed
- 3 tbsp curry paste
- 2 tbsp fresh chopped coriander + extra for garnish
- 250ml/1 cup passata/sieved tomatoes
- Salt & pepper to taste

1 Add all the ingredients to the slow cooker, cover and leave to cook on low for 1-2 hours or until the prawns are cooked through and the peas are tender.

2 Sprinkle with chopped coriander and serve with rice.

This is a really simple 'cheat' curry using curry paste. If you want a slightly different taste you could use less passata and add a little coconut milk to the recipe after cooking.

FISH STEW

SERVES 4 CALORIES PER SERVING 245

- 450g/1lb white fish fillets, cubed
- 1 leek, chopped
- 4 garlic cloves, crushed
- 1 400g/14oz tin chopped tomatoes
- 100g/3½ oz frozen peas
- 2 celery stalks, chopped
- 1 onion chopped
- ½ tsp fennel seeds
- 1 tbsp dried basil
- 1lt/4 cups fish stock
- 250g/9oz raw prawns
- Salt & Pepper to taste

1 Mix together all the ingredients, except the fish, peas and prawns in the slow cooker. Season, cover and leave to cook on low for 4-5 hours or high for 2-3 hours.

2 Meanwhile season the fish and prawns. 45 mins before the end of cooking add the fish, prawns and peas. Continue to cook until the seafood is cooked right through and the peas are tender.

3 Serve with noodles as a soup stew.

Feel free to use any type of meaty white fish you like and, if you feel adventurous, you could add some squid, octopus or clams to the stew.

FRESH MACKEREL & PEPPERS

SERVES 4 CALORIES PER SERVING 190

- 2 yellow or orange peppers, sliced
- 2 onions, sliced
- 1 garlic clove, crushed
- 1 red chilli, finely sliced
- 250ml/1 cup fish stock
- 400g/14oz fresh whole mackerel, gutted
- 200g/7oz ripe plum tomatoes, chopped
- 2 tbsp tomato puree
- 200g/7oz rocket
- Low cal cooking oil spray
- Salt & pepper to taste

1 Gently sauté the peppers, onions, garlic & chilli in a little low cal spray until softened.

2 Add the sautéed vegetables to the slow cooker along with all the other ingredients, except the rocket.

3 Gently combine, cover and leave to cook on low for 4-6 hours or until the fish is tender and cooked through.

4 Gently lift out of the slow cooker (try to keep the fish whole), season and serve with the rocket leaves.

Use yellow or orange peppers rather than un-ripened green peppers.

FRESH HERBED SALMON

SERVES 4 · CALORIES PER SERVING 250

- 500g/1lb 2oz boneless salmon fillets
- 250ml/1 cup fish stock
- 4 tbsp freshly chopped flat leaf parsley
- 4 tbsp freshly chopped basil
- 3 tbsp low fat mayonnaise
- Lemon wedges to serve
- 200g/7oz mixed green salad leaves
- Low cal cooking oil spray
- Salt & pepper to taste

1 Place the salmon, stock and half the chopped herbs in the slow cooker. Gently combine, cover and leave to cook on high for 1-2 hours or until the fish is tender and cooked through.

2 Mix the rest of the chopped herbs together with the mayonnaise, a squeeze of lemon and some salt & pepper.

3 Remove the salmon fillets from the slow cooker.

4 Spread the herbed mayonnaise onto the salmon fillets and serve with salad leaves and lemon wedges to serve.

You can alter the mix of fresh herbs to suit your own taste. Chives and coriander make a good alternative.

CARIBBEAN SPICED SCALLOPS

SERVES 4 · CALORIES PER SERVING 200

- 200g/7oz ripe plum tomatoes, roughly chopped
- 500g/1lb 2oz prepared fresh scallops
- 250ml/1 cup fish stock
- ½ tsp each ground all spice, chilli powder, coriander & paprika
- 1 bunch spring onions, roughly chopped
- 2 large romaine lettuces, shredded
- 2 red peppers, sliced
- Low cal cooking oil spray
- Salt & pepper to taste

1 First gently sauté the peppers & plum tomatoes in a little low cal oil for a few minutes until softened.

2 Place the scallops, stock, dried spices, spring onions, sautéed peppers & plum tomatoes in the slow cooker.

3 Gently combine, cover and leave to cook on high for 45 minutes - 1 hour or until the scallops are cooked through.

4 Gently lift the scallops, tomatoes & peppers out of the slow cooker.

5 Season and serve with the shredded lettuce.

Sweet potato mash makes a great side to this Caribbean dish.

LIME SHRIMPS, BABY SPINACH & RICE

SERVES 4 · CALORIES PER SERVING 280

- 500g/1lb 2oz raw shelled king prawns
- 250ml/1 cup low fat coconut milk
- 2 tbsp lime juice
- 1 tbsp Thai fish sauce
- 1 tsp brown sugar
- 1 red chilli, finely sliced
- 200g/7oz baby spinach leaves
- 4 tbsp freshly chopped coriander
- 200g/7oz long grain rice
- Low cal cooking oil spray
- Salt & pepper to taste

1 Place the prawns, coconut milk, lime juice, fish sauce, sugar, chilli & spinach in the slow cooker.

2 Gently combine, cover and leave to cook on high for 45 minutes - 1 hour or until the prawns are cooked through.

3 Meanwhile cook the rice in salted boiling water until tender.

4 Serve the prawns and coconut milk on top of the drained rice with freshly chopped coriander sprinkled on top.

Spinach is in season throughout late spring and summer. Baby leaves are the most sweet and tender.

SUGAR SNAP PINEAPPLE PRAWNS

SERVES 4 · CALORIES PER SERVING 360

- 1 onion, sliced
- 2 garlic cloves, crushed
- 500g/1lb 2oz raw shelled king prawns
- 250ml/1 cup low fat coconut milk
- 1 tbsp medium curry powder
- 1 tbsp lime juice
- 1 tbsp Thai fish sauce
- 2 tbsp tomato puree
- 200g/7oz fresh or tinned pineapple, roughly chopped
- 200g/7oz sugar snap peas
- 200g/7oz fine egg noodles
- Low cal cooking oil spray
- Salt & pepper to taste

1 Gently sauté the onions & garlic in a little low cal oil for a few minutes until softened. Then place in the slow cooker.

2 Add the prawns, coconut milk, curry powder, lime juice, fish sauce, tomato puree, pineapple & peas in the slow cooker.

3 Gently combine, cover and leave to cook on high for 1-2 hours or until the prawns are cooked through.

4 Meanwhile cook the noodles in salted boiling water until tender.

5 Mix the drained noodles, prawns and sauce together & serve.

You could serve the sugar snaps peas roughly chopped and raw in this lovely summer noodle dish if you prefer.

FENNEL RISOTTO

SERVES 3   CALORIES PER SERVING 355

- 1 fennel bulb, diced
- 250g/9oz risotto rice
- 1 carrot, chopped
- 1 onion, chopped
- 25g/1oz grated parmesan cheese
- 50g/2oz black olives, finely chopped
- 3 garlic cloves, crushed
- 1lt/4 cups vegetable stock
- 125g/4oz frozen peas
- 50g/2oz rocket
- 15g/ ½ oz butter
- Salt & pepper to taste

1 Preheat the slow cooker and place the butter in the bottom. When it is melted, add the risotto rice and stir well until every grain is finely coated. Add the rest of the ingredients, except the cheese and rocket, to the slow cooker and season well. Cover and leave to cook on high for 2-3 hours. If you need more liquid during cooking go ahead by adding just a little each time.

2 After cooking, all the liquid should be absorbed and the rice should be tender. If it isn't, leave to cook for a little longer with the lid off.

3 Serve sprinkled with parmesan cheese and the rocket piled on top.

Risotto usually needs a lot of stirring during cooking. This slow cooker alternative is a great labour saver with virtually no stirring required.

WILD MUSHROOM STROGANOFF

SERVES 4   CALORIES PER SERVING 101

- 500g/1lb 2oz wild mixed mushrooms sliced
- 2 onions, chopped
- 4 garlic cloves, crushed
- 2 tsp smoked paprika
- 250ml/1 cup vegetable stock
- 1 400g/14oz tin low fat condensed mushroom soup
- Bunch flat chopped leaf parsley (reserve a little for garnish)

1 Add all the ingredients into the slow cooker. Close the lid tightly and leave to cook on high for 2-3 hours or low for 4-5 hours. Ensure the mushrooms are tender and serve with pasta or rice and a spoon of fat free Greek yoghurt.

The more exciting the mushrooms the better this dish is going to taste. Use whatever you can get your hands on but a combination of portobello, shitake, morel, oyster and enoki would be fantastic. However don't be put off if you can only get regular varieties - it will still taste great!

BEAN, POTATO & CHEESE STEW

SERVES 4 — CALORIES PER SERVING 434

- 1 400g/14oz tin sweetcorn
- 2 400g/14oz tins mixed beans, drained
- 1 red (bell) pepper, chopped
- 1 onion, chopped
- 500ml/2 cups passata/sieved tomatoes
- 1 tsp each cumin & coriander
- 125g/4oz grated low fat cheese
- 125g/4oz potatoes, diced & peeled
- ½ tsp cayenne pepper
- Juice of one lemon or 2tbsp lemon juice
- Salt & pepper to taste

1 Add all the ingredients to the slow cooker, except the cheese. Combine well and sprinkle the cheese onto the top. Cook on low for 5-6 hours or on high for 3-4 hours with the lid tightly shut.

2 Make sure the potatoes are tender and serve with sour cream and flat bread. If you find the stew is a little dry during cooking, add some water to loosen.

This vegetarian meal is a lovely Mexican inspired dish which is so hearty you won't miss the meat at all. Feel free to spice it up with extra cayenne pepper if you like and serve with an onion & tomato or green salad.

LENTIL DHAL

SERVES 4 — CALORIES PER SERVING 160

- 400g/14oz split red lentils
- 1 onion, chopped
- 1 garlic clove, crushed
- 500ml/2 cups vegetable stock
- 1 tsp each ground coriander, turmeric & cumin
- ½ each tsp ground ginger, paprika & mustard seeds
- 2 tbsp freshly chopped coriander
- 25g/1oz butter
- Salt & pepper to taste

1 Add all the ingredients, except corriander to the slow cooker, cover and leave to cook on low for 4-6 hours or until the lentils are tender and the liquid absorbed. Add a little more stock or water during cooking if needed. If there is too much liquid, take the lid off and leave to cook on high for approx 40 mins.

2 Sprinkle the chopped coriander over the top and serve.

Dhal is a one of the most common dishes in Asia. It is eaten by some families at almost every single meal time. This simple version is great served with Indian chapatti bread.

BUTTER BEAN & ALMOND STEW

SERVES 4 CALORIES PER SERVING 206

- 1 onion, sliced into rounds
- 2 garlic cloves, crushed
- 300g/11oz new potatoes, sliced
- 1 tsp mustard seeds
- 2 tbsp tomato puree/paste
- ½ tsp ground cinnamon
- 1 celery stick, chopped
- 450g/1lb cauliflower florets
- 50g/2oz sultanas
- 200g/7oz tinned butter beans, drained
- 50g/2oz chopped almonds
- 1 400g/14oz tin chopped tomatoes
- 250ml/1 cup vegetable stock
- Salt & pepper to taste

1 Add all the ingredients to the slow cooker, cover, stir well and leave to cook on high for 2-3 hours or low for 4-5 hours or until the vegetables are tender.

If you want the stew a little thicker, take the lid off and continue to cook on high for 45mins or until the consistency is to your liking.

SUMMER CRUSTLESS QUICHE

SERVES 4 CALORIES PER SERVING 200

- 200g/7oz cherry tomatoes, halved
- 1 red pepper, sliced
- 1 yellow pepper, sliced
- 125g/4oz courgettes, diced
- 125g/4oz aubergine/egg plant, diced
- 125g/4oz peas
- 2 garlic cloves, crushed
- 1 tsp dried mixed herbs
- 1 onion, sliced
- 6 free range eggs
- 200g/7oz rocket
- Low cal cooking oil spray
- Salt & pepper to taste

1 Place the tomatoes, peppers, courgettes, aubergines, peas, garlic, herbs & sliced onions in the slow cooker. Spray well with a little low cal cooking oil. Combine, cover and leave to cook on high for 2 hours.

2 Break the eggs into a bowl, gently whisk and pour into the slow cooker.

3 Quickly combine for a few seconds. Replace the lid and leave to cook for a further 1-1½ hours or until the eggs are set and the vegetables are tender.

4 Gently lift out of the slow cooker.

5 Slice into thick wedges and serve with the rocket leaves.

This type of crust-less quiche is popular in Italy. Use whichever vegetables you have to hand to create your own version.

MUSHROOMS & DOLCELATTE CHEESE

SERVES 4 CALORIES PER SERVING 90

- 600g/1lb 5oz portabella mushrooms, thickly sliced
- 2 garlic cloves, crushed
- 60ml/¼ cup vegetable stock
- 1 tbsp lemon juice
- 50g/2oz dolcelatte cheese
- 2 tbsp freshly chopped basil
- Low cal cooking oil spray
- Salt & pepper to taste

1 **Place the mushrooms, garlic, stock & lemon juice in the slow cooker.**

2 **Combine, cover and leave to cook on high for 2-4 hours or until most of the liquid has disappeared.**

3 **Stir in the dolcelatte cheese and fresh basil.**

4 **Check the seasoning and serve.**

These delicious mushrooms can be served as a luxurious side dish, on top of French toast or tossed through long cut spaghetti.

VEGGIE RATATOUILLE

SERVES 4 CALORIES PER SERVING 120

- 200g/7oz sugar snap peas
- 200g/7oz baby courgettes, sliced lengthways
- 200g/7oz baby sweetcorn, sliced lengthways
- 1 aubergine, diced
- 2 yellow peppers, sliced
- 2 garlic cloves, crushed
- 1 vegetable stock cube, crumbled
- 800g/1¾lb tinned chopped tomatoes
- 1 tbsp tomato puree/paste
- 2 tbsp each freshly chopped basil & flat leaf parsley
- Salt & pepper to taste

1 **Place all the ingredients in the slow cooker.**

2 **Cover and leave to cook on high for 3-4 hours / low for 6-8 hours, or until the vegetables are tender.**

3 **Check the seasoning and serve.**

Of course you could also use fresh tomatoes rather than chopped tomatoes if you have enough to hand.

PAPRIKA SWEET POTATOES

SERVES 4 · CALORIES PER SERVING 190

- 500g/1lb 2oz sweet potatoes, cut into 4cm cubes
- 1 tsp paprika
- 1 red chilli, finely chopped
- 1 red onion, sliced
- 2 yellow peppers, sliced
- 2 garlic cloves, crushed
- 1 vegetable stock cube, crumbled
- 250ml/1 cup tomato passata/sieved tomatoes
- 400g/14oz tinned chopped tomatoes
- ½ tsp brown sugar
- 1 tbsp tomato puree/paste
- Salt & pepper to taste

1 Place all the ingredients in the slow cooker.

2 Cover and leave to cook on high for 3-4 hours or until the sweet potatoes are tender but not falling apart.

3 Check the seasoning and serve.

The sugar and seasoning will balance the acidity of the tomatoes, add a little more if needed.

BABY SPINACH & SPICED CHICKPEAS

SERVES 4 · CALORIES PER SERVING 175

- 300g/11oz baby spinach leaves
- 400g/14oz tinned chickpeas, drained
- 400g/14oz fresh ripe tomatoes, roughly chopped
- 1 onion, sliced
- 2 garlic cloves, crushed
- 1 tbsp medium or hot curry powder
- 60ml/¼ cup vegetable stock
- 4 tbsp fat free Greek yoghurt
- Salt & pepper to taste

1 Place all the ingredients, except the Greek yoghurt, in the slow cooker.

2 Cover and leave to cook on low for 3-4 hours (add a little more stock during cooking if needed).

3 Check the seasoning and serve with a dollop of Greek yoghurt on the side.

Add some chopped red chillies to garnish this dish if you like.

SLOW COOKED SUMMER PEPPERS

- SERVES 4
- CALORIES PER SERVING 150

- 8 red, yellow or orange peppers, quartered
- 200g/7oz vine ripened tomatoes, halved
- 8 unpeeled garlic cloves
- 2 tsp brown sugar
- 2 tbsp olive oil
- Salt & pepper to taste

1 Place all the ingredients in the slow cooker. Cover and leave to cook on low for 6-8 (add a splash of water during cooking if needed).

2 Check the seasoning and serve.

3 If you love garlic you can squeeze the garlic pulp out of the cloves and mix with the peppers too.

Don't use green peppers as they can have a bitter taste which doesn't complement this recipe. Eat these slow cooked peppers just as they are or serve with salad, boiled rice or green salad.

MOZZARELLA & BASIL TOMATOES

- SERVES 4
- CALORIES PER SERVING 130

- 1 tbsp olive oil
- 2 garlic cloves, crushed
- 1 tsp brown sugar
- 2 tsp balsamic vinegar
- 8 large beef tomatoes
- 3 tbsp water
- 100g/3½oz low fat mozzarella cheese, roughly chopped
- 3 tbsp freshly chopped basil
- Salt & pepper to taste

1 Mix the oil, garlic, sugar & balsamic vinegar together.

2 Halve the tomatoes and brush with the sweet garlic oil.

3 Place in the slow cooker, with the water, cover and leave to cook on low for 4-6 hours (add a little more water during cooking if needed).

4 When the tomatoes are tender sprinkle each on top with mozzarella cheese and continue cooking until the cheese melts.

5 Remove from the slow cooker, sprinkle with basil and serve.

Cook the tomatoes long enough for them to be super-tender but not so that they lose their form and fall apart.

SMOKY BEANS & SPRING ONIONS

SERVES 4 CALORIES PER SERVING 250

- 1 large bunch spring onions
- 3 tbsp freshly chopped flat leaf parsley
- 800g/1¾lb tinned pinto beans, drained & rinsed
- 1 tbsp tomato puree/paste
- 1 tsp brown sugar
- 120ml/½ cup vegetable stock
- 200g/7oz shop bought roasted peppers, roughly chopped
- 1 tbsp smoked paprika
- 1 garlic clove, crushed
- Salt & pepper to taste

1 Slice the spring onions diagonally, mix with the chopped parsley and put to one side.

2 Add the drained pinto beans, puree, sugar, peppers, stock, paprika & garlic to the slow cooker. Cover and leave to cook on high for 2-4 hours or until the stock has reduced and the smoky beans are tender.

3 Remove from the slow cooker and divide into bowls.

4 Check the seasoning, sprinkle with the fresh parsley & spring onion mix and serve.

Pinto beans are a staple of Mexican cooking. Garnishing with fresh spring onions gives this dish a light crunchy bite.

CAJUN SPRING GREENS

SERVES 4 CALORIES PER SERVING 90

- 1 tbsp Cajun seasoning (or make your own by mixing ½ tsp each paprika, cayenne pepper, sea salt, black pepper, cumin & ground garlic)
- 1 garlic clove, crushed
- 500g/1lb 2oz shredded spring greens
- 250ml/1 cup vegetable stock
- Lemon wedges to serve
- Salt & pepper to taste

1 Add the spring greens, stock, Cajun seasoning & garlic to the slow cooker.

2 Cover and leave to cook on high for 2-4 hours or until the stock has reduced and the spring greens are tender.

3 Remove from the slow cooker, drain any stock, check the seasoning and serve with lemon wedges.

Handy bags of prepared shredded spring greens are readily available in most supermarkets.

SWEET ROASTED VEGETABLES

SERVES 4 · CALORIES PER SERVING 150

- 200g/7oz carrots, thickly sliced
- 200g/7oz sweet potatoes, thickly sliced
- 200g/7oz parsnips, thickly sliced
- 200g/7oz cherry tomatoes, halved
- 200g/7oz baby sweetcorn, sliced lengthways
- 1 red onion, quartered and divided into segments
- 1 red pepper, sliced
- 1 tbsp runny honey
- 1 tbsp balsamic vinegar
- 1 tbsp olive oil
- 1 tbsp water
- 1 tsp dried basil or mixed herbs
- Salt & pepper to taste

1 Add all the ingredients to the slow cooker and combine really well to make sure all the vegetables are properly coated.

2 Cover and leave to cook on low for 4-6 hours or until all the vegetables are tender (add a splash of water during cooking if needed).

3 Remove from the slow cooker, check the seasoning and serve.

This colourful roasted vegetable medley is a meal on its own or you could serve with a mixed salad.

SLOW SPANISH TOMBET

SERVES 4 · CALORIES PER SERVING 115

- 2 fresh aubergines/eggplant, cubed
- 2 courgettes , cut into strips
- 200g/7oz fresh tomatoes, cubed
- 2 (bell) peppers, sliced
- 5 tbsp tomato puree/paste
- 2 large red onions, 1 chopped, 1 sliced
- 1 tsp each of dried marjoram, basil & thyme
- 1 tsp paprika
- 1 tsp capers, chopped
- Handful pitted black olives, chopped
- 3 garlic cloves, crushed
- 250ml/1 cup vegetable stock
- 1 tsp salt
- 1 tsp sugar
- 1 tbsp olive oil
- 3 tbsp freshly chopped basil

1 Combine all ingredients, except the fresh basil, in the slow cooker, cover and leave to cook on low for 4-5 hours or high for 2-3 hours.

2 Add a little more stock during cooking if needed, or if it needs thickening remove the lid and leave to cook on high for a further 45 minutes or until you get the desired consistency.

3 Garnish with the finely chopped basil and serve.

Tombet is the Spanish version of the French classic ratatouille. This is lovely served with Spanish toast; which is simply rough cut farmhouse bread toasted and rubbed with garlic, salt & olive oil.

CARIBBEAN SPICED SWEET POTATOES

SERVES 4 CALORIES PER SERVING 225

- 400g/14oz sweet potatoes,
- cubed
- 1 onion, chopped
- 125g/4oz green beans, sliced
- 1 200g/7oz tin black beans
- ½ cup /120ml vegetable stock
- ½ cup/120ml coconut milk
- 2 garlic cloves, crushed
- ½ tsp each cayenne pepper,
- nutmeg, cinnamon
- 1 tsp each dried onion powder,
- thyme, parsley, paprika &
- brown sugar
- Salt & pepper to taste

1 Combine all ingredients in the slow cooker. Cover and leave to cook on low for 4-6 hours or until the sweet potatoes are tender.

2 Add a little more stock during cooking if needed, or if it needs thickening remove the lid and leave to cook on high for a further 45 minutes or until you get the desired consistency.

For an authentic taste of the Caribbean serve with fried plantain and chunky coleslaw.

SHEPHERD-LESS LENTIL PIE

SERVES 4 CALORIES PER SERVING 250

- 1 tbsp olive oil
- 1 onions, chopped
- 2 carrots, diced
- 2 stalks celery, chopped
- 1 garlic clove, crushed
- 75g/3oz mushrooms , sliced
- 1 bay leaf
- 1 tbsp dried thyme
- 100g/3 ½ oz dried green lentils (soaked overnight)
- 60ml/ ¼ cup red wine
- 2 tbsp vegetarian worcestershire sauce
- 250ml/1 cup vegetable stock
- 3 tbsp tomato purée
- 1 ½ lb / 680g mashed potato to top the pie

1 Gently sauté the onions, celery, carrots, garlic and herbs in the oil for a few minutes. Remove to the slow cooker and combine well with all the other ingredients, except the mashed potato.

2 Season, cover and leave to cook on low for 4-5 hours or high for 2-3 hours.

3 Add a little more stock during cooking if needed, or if it needs thickening remove the lid and leave to cook on high for a further 45 minutes or until you get the desired consistency.

4 Remove from the slow cooker and place in an ovenproof dish. Top with the mashed potato and brown under the grill for a few minutes.

Lovely served with peas and spring greens dressed with garlic oil.

SLOPPY JOES

SERVES 4 · CALORIES PER SERVING 160

- 200g/7oz lentils (soaked overnight)
- 1 400g/14oz tin chopped tomatoes
- 1 tsp olive oil
- 1 onion, chopped
- 1 green pepper, chopped
- 1 tsp chilli powder
- ½ tsp garlic powder
- ½ tsp mustard powder
- 250ml/1 cup vegetable stock
- 2 tbsp soy sauce
- 125g/4oz soy meat (TVP / Quorn mince)
- 3 tbsp ketchup or BBQ sauce
- Salt & pepper to taste

1 Gently sauté the onions & pepper in a frying pan with the oil for a few minutes then combine all the ingredients into the slow cooker, cover and cook on low for 6-8 hours or until the lentils are tender.

2 Add a little more stock during cooking if needed, or if it needs thickening remove the lid and leave to cook on high for a further 45 minutes or until you get the desired consistency.

3 Serve with toasted sandwich buns, lettuce & onion.

An American classic, 'Sloppy Joes' can still be enjoyed by the meat-free amongst us. This recipe uses soy meat but that could be substituted for a basic bean mix; soak overnight whatever store cupboard beans you have and fry them with some garlic, onion and a little flaxseed.

LUXURY MACARONI CHEESE

SERVES 4 · CALORIES PER SERVING 380

- 300g/11oz macaroni pasta
- 200g/7oz grated vegetarian reduced fat cheddar cheese
- 2 tsp dijon mustard
- 120ml/ ½ cup evaporated milk
- 385ml/1 ½ cups semi skimmed milk
- 2 free range eggs, beaten
- 1 tsp low fat 'butter' spread
- ½ tsp paprika
- ½ tsp ground nutmeg

1 Combine all the ingredients, except the nutmeg, in the slow cooker. Cover and leave to cook on low for 3-4 hours or high for 2-3 hours. Make sure the pasta is tender. Add more milk if needed and stir well. Sprinkle with nutmeg before serving.

Using the evaporated milk in this recipe makes for a lovely, creamy consistency. Mare sure you don't overcook the macaroni.

BEETROOT BEAN SALAD TOPPING

SERVES 4 · CALORIES PER SERVING 195

- 1 onion, chopped
- 450g/1lb fresh raw beetroot, cubed
- 2 400g/14oz tins cannellini beans, drained
- 375ml/1½ cups vegetable stock
- 3 tbsp fresh chopped coriander
- Salt & pepper to taste

1 Gently sauté the onions in a little low cal spray for a few minutes until soft. Add all the ingredients to the slow cooker and gently combine.

2 Cover, season and leave to cook on low for 3-5 hours or until everything is tender and cooked through. Add a little more stock during cooking if needed.

3 Serve with green salad, red onions & Greek yoghurt.

Fresh beetroot is a much overlooked ingredient which, if given a chance, can form the heart of a good meal.

SPICED SWEET POTATOES & EGGS

SERVES 4 · CALORIES PER SERVING 271

- 1 onion, chopped
- 1 tsp each ground cumin, coriander & turmeric
- ½ tsp each chilli power, crushed chilli flakes & garam masala
- 1 400g/14oz tins chopped tomatoes
- 250ml/1 cup vegetable stock
- 300g/11oz sweet potatoes, peeled & cubed
- 60ml/¼ cup single cream
- 4 free range eggs, hard-boiled, peeled and quartered
- 3 garlic cloves, crushed
- 200g/7oz lentils, soaked overnight
- 1 tsp brown sugar
- 100g/3½ oz peas
- 100g/3½ oz baby sweetcorn
- Low cal cooking spray
- Salt & pepper to taste

1 Gently sauté the onions in a little low cal spray for a few minutes until soft. Add all the ingredients to the slow cooker, except the cream and eggs, and gently combine.

2 Cover, season and leave to cook on low for 5-7 hours or until everything is tender and cooked through.

3 10 minutes before serving add the eggs and cream and gently stir through.

4 Serve with rice or flat bread and salad.

If you prefer, you can use your eggs in a different way by breaking them raw into the slow cooker half an hour before the end of cooking so that they set whole in the dish.

KALE & LENTIL SUPPER

SERVES 4 CALORIES PER SERVING 170

- 200g/7oz kale, shredded
- 1 tsp olive oil
- 300g/11oz lentils
- 1 onion, chopped
- 4 garlic cloves, crushed
- 3 roasted red peppers, sliced (shop bought)
- 1 400g/14oz tin chopped tomatoes
- ½ tsp sea salt
- 1 tsp each, ginger, cumin & coriander
- 250ml/1 cups vegetable stock
- Salt & pepper to taste

1 Add all the ingredients into the slow cooker. Season, cover and leave to cook on low for 4-6 hours or until the lentils are tender and the stock absorbed. Add a little more stock during cooking if needed.

Kale is a real super-food which has enjoyed a massive surge in popularity in recent years. It can be a little tough but slow cooking counteracts this beautifully.

GARLIC & BROCCOLI CRUMB PASTA

SERVES 4 CALORIES PER SERVING 208

- 300g/11oz fusilli pasta
- 600g/1lb 5oz tenderstem broccoli, chopped
- 3 cloves garlic, crushed
- 1 tsp olive oil
- 60ml/¼ cup vegetable stock
- ¼ tsp crushed chilli flakes (or more to taste)
- 1 slice bread
- 3 tbsp lemon juice
- Salt & pepper to taste

1 Place the broccoli, garlic, lemon juice and stock in the slow cooker and combine well. Cover, season and leave to cook on high for 1-3 hours or until tender.

2 Meanwhile cook the pasta in salted boiling water until tender, then drain.

3 Place the bread in a food processor and whizz to make breadcrumbs. Heat the oil in a frying pan and fry the breadcrumbs until crispy.

4 Combine the cooked broccoli and pasta together. Season well, sprinkle with the breadcrumbs and serve.

You could also add some lemon zest to the breadcrumbs when they are frying for an extra citrus burst.

CHICKEN, BACON AND BEER

SERVES 6 · CALORIES PER SERVING 410

- 5 rashers back bacon
- 3 tbsp all-purpose gluten-free flour
- 1kg/2¼lb boneless, skinless chicken thighs
- 370ml/1½ cups gluten-free beer
- 120ml/½ cup gluten free hot chicken stock
- 2 tbsp barbecue sauce
- 1 tsp dried oregano
- ½ tsp dried thyme
- ¼ tsp sea salt
- ¼ tsp freshly ground pepper
- 1 tbsp water
- 2 tsp tapioca or arrowroot starch

1 Cook the bacon under the grill until crispy. Leave to cool and chop finely.

2 Toss the chicken thighs in the flour until coated, then place in the bottom of the slow cooker.

3 In a bowl, mix together the bacon pieces, beer, stock, barbecue sauce and herbs. Then pour the mixture over the chicken in the slow cooker. Cover and cook on Low for 8-9 hours or High for 4-5 hours. Ensure the chicken it cooked through.

4 Combine the water and starch in a small bowl to make a smooth paste. Set aside.

5 Remove the chicken with a slotted spoon and place in a bowl. Cover with foil to keep warm.

6 Stir the starch mixture in with leftover chicken liquids in the slow cooker. Whisk until combined. Cover and cook, on Low, for 15 minutes to make a 'gravy'.

7 Drizzle the gravy over the chicken and serve.

SATSUMA CHICKEN

SERVES 6 · CALORIES PER SERVING 394

- 6 skin-on chicken thighs
- 2 tsp Chinese Five Spice
- ½ tsp salt
- 225g/8oz satsuma slices
- 2 garlic cloves, crushed
- 1 tbsp grated ginger
- ½ red chilli, seeded & finely chopped
- 1 tbsp lime juice
- 1 tbsp brown sugar
- 1 tsp sesame oil
- 2 tbsp fish sauce

1 Rub the chicken thighs with the five spice powder and salt.

2 In a hot frying pan, sear the chicken for about 3 minutes on each side.

3 Lay the chicken in the slow cooker, skin side up. Combine the rest of the ingredients in a small bowl and mix well. Pour this over the chicken in the slow cooker.

4 Cook on High for 4 hours, or Low for 6 hours. Check the chicken is tender and cooked through, and then remove to a serving dish.

5 Use a hand blender to puree the sauce in the bottom of the slow cooker, or spoon it into a blender.

6 Whizz until the sauce is smooth then pour it over the chicken. Serve warm.

CHICKEN ENCHILADAS

SERVES 6 CALORIES PER SERVING 490

- 250g/9oz chicken breast, cooked & shredded
- 400g/14oz tin black beans, rinsed & drained
- 1 tsp olive oil
- 1 medium onion, peeled & chopped
- 1 red chilli seeded & chopped
- 2 cloves garlic, crushed
- 1 tsp chilli powder
- 400g/14oz tin chopped tomatoes, drained
- 225g/8oz tin tomato passata/sieved tomatoes
- 1 tsp dried mixed herbs
- Cooking spray
- 175g/6oz sweetcorn
- 5 gluten free soft tortillas
- 225g/8oz reduced-fat mature Cheddar cheese, grated
- Coriander sprigs, to garnish

1 Heat the olive oil in a large pan over medium-high heat. Add the onion, chopped chilli & garlic and gently sauté for a few minutes. Stir in the chilli powder, tomatoes and passata.

2 Coat the slow cooker with cooking spray. Spread 3 tbsp of the tomato mixture from the pan onto the bottom of the slow cooker. Combine the remaining tomato mixture with the chicken, corn, and beans.

3 Place one tortilla on top of the sauce in slow cooker. Layer on the chicken mixture, some cheese, another tortilla and so on, finishing with cheese.

4 Cover and cook on Low for 2 hours or until the cheese melts and the edges are lightly browned. Serve cut into 8 wedges and garnished with the coriander sprigs.

EASY SAUSAGE AND BEAN CASSEROLE

SERVES 4 CALORIES PER SERVING 357

- 8 gluten free sausages
- 2 x 400g/14oz tins mixed beans
- 2 x 400g/14oz tins chopped tomato
- 1 tsp dried basil
- 2 tsp dried oregano
- 1 tbsp sugar
- Salt and pepper

1 Brown the sausages in a non-stick frying pan over a high heat for 3-5 minutes. Transfer them to the slow cooker and add the beans.

2 Add one tin of tomatoes to the slow cooker. Drain the other tin and pour the tomatoes without the juice into the slow cooker. Stir in the herbs and sugar cover and cook on Low for up to 6-8 hours or until the sausages are cooked through and piping hot.

Adding a little sugar brings out the natural sweetness of tomatoes.

SPICED PORK RIBS

SERVES 4 CALORIES PER SERVING 415

- 1½kg/3lb 6oz pork ribs
- 250ml/1 cup gluten free barbecue sauce (use only half in the slow cooker)
- 2 gluten free stock cubes
- 2 bay leaves
- 1 tsp coriander seeds
- 1 tsp mustard seeds
- 1 tsp peppercorns
- 1½lt/6 cups water

1 Add all the ingredients to the slow cooker (using only half the barbecue sauce). Top up with enough water to cover the ribs (around 1½lt). Cook on Low for around 8 hours until the meat is very tender but not completely falling off the bone.

2 Heat the oven to 220C/200C Fan. Carefully remove the ribs from the slow cooker using a slotted spoon or tongs. Baste them with the remaining barbecue sauce and lay them on a foil-lined baking tray. Cook for 20–30 minutes until starting to crisp.

You can cook the ribs in the slow cooker the day before, baste them in barbecue sauce, cover and refrigerate overnight before either oven-cooking or barbecuing them.

COCONUT BEEF CURRY

SERVES 4 CALORIES PER SERVING 497

- 1 tbsp peanut oil
- 900g/2lb beef brisket, cut into large chunks
- 25g/1oz coriander
- 1 stalk lemongrass, roughly chopped
- 2 cloves garlic, peeled & chopped
- 1 small green chilli, seeded & chopped
- 1 tsp fresh grated ginger
- 1 tbsp rice wine vinegar
- 1 tbsp fish sauce
- 1 tbsp brown sugar
- 250ml/1 cup light coconut milk
- 1 star anise
- 3 kaffir lime leaves
- 1 tbsp lime juice

1 Switch the slow cooker on to High.

2 Heat a little of the oil in a large pan and brown the beef.

3 Combine half the coriander, the lemongrass, garlic and chillies with the rest of the oil until you have a rough paste.

4 Heat the paste in the pan for a few minutes, then add the beef and all the remaining ingredients (apart from the left over coriander and lime juice).

5 Turn the slow cooker down to Low and cook for 8 hrs, or until the meat is very tender. Stir in the remaining coriander and lime juice, then season with more fish sauce.

If you like, use beef ribs instead of brisket, and pull the meat from the bone after cooking.

SPICY CHICKEN AND TOMATO STEW

- SERVES 4
- CALORIES PER SERVING 204

- 1 tbsp vegetable oil
- 1 medium onion, finely chopped
- 3 cloves garlic, crushed
- ½ tsp brown sugar
- 1 tsp chilli paste
- 400g/14oz tin chopped tomatoes
- 500g/1lb skinless chicken breasts
- 1 red onion, sliced into rings
- 1 tbsp chopped coriander leaves

1 Heat the oil in a medium saucepan. Add the onion & garlic and gently sauté for 5 minutes until softened.

2 Add to the slow cooker and stir in the sugar, chilli paste, tomatoes and chicken. Cover and cook on High for 2-3 hours or until the chicken is cooked through.

3 Remove the chicken and shred with 2 forks, then stir back into the sauce. Scatter with the red onion rings and coriander.

Serve with rice, or with corn tortillas.

BOLOGNESE

- SERVES 6
- CALORIES PER SERVING 355

- 2 tbsp olive oil
- 3 rashers smoked back bacon, chopped
- 750g/1lb 11oz lean minced beef
- 2 onions, peeled & finely chopped
- 1 large carrot, peeled & finely chopped
- 2 stalks celery, finely chopped
- 250g/9oz mushrooms, sliced
- 4 cloves garlic, crushed
- 1 tbsp dried mixed herbs
- 1 bay leaf
- 3 x 400g/14oz tins chopped tomatoes
- 2 tbsp tomato purée/paste
- 2 tbsp red wine vinegar
- ½ tbsp sugar
- Salt and pepper

1 Heat the oil in a large frying pan. Fry the bacon and brown the mince, then tip it all into the slow cooker. Add the vegetables, garlic, herbs, tomatoes, tomato purée, wine, vinegar, sugar and seasoning.

2 Cover and cook on Low for 6-8 hours, then uncover, turn up to High and cook for another hour until thick.

Serve with gluten free spaghetti and grated parmesan.

PORK AND PLUM CASSEROLE

SERVES 4 · CALORIES PER SERVING 496

- 750g/1lb 11oz pork shoulder
- 2 tbsp rice wine
- 3 tbsp gluten free soy sauce
- 1 tsp grated root ginger
- 3 cloves garlic, crushed
- ½ red chilli, seeded & finely chopped
- 1 tbsp vegetable oil
- 3 spring onions, finely sliced
- 1 star anise
- 1 tsp five-spice powder
- 1 cinnamon stick
- 1 tbsp sugar
- 1 tbsp tomato purée
- 250ml/1 cup gluten free hot chicken stock
- 4 ripe plums, stoned & chopped

1 Cut the pork into approximately 4cm/2-inch cubes. Place in a bowl and add the wine, soy sauce, half the ginger, half the garlic and half the chilli. Marinate for at least 1 hour, or up to 24 hours.

2 Heat the vegetable oil in a large pan gently sauté the spring onions, the remaining ginger, garlic, chilli, cinnamon, star anise, five-spice, sugar and tomato purée. When the onions are soft, remove to a plate. Increase the heat, add the pork and quickly fry each side until sealed.

3 Tip everything into the slow cooker. Cover and cook on Low for 8-9 hours. Skim off any surface fat and about an hour before the end of cooking, stir in the plums.

4 Scatter the remaining spring onions over the top, and serve.

The pork should be super-tender after this extended period of slow cooking.

BACON AND CHICKEN STEW

SERVES 6 · CALORIES PER SERVING 325

- 1 tbsp olive oil
- 6 chicken thighs, skinless
- 12 rashers smoked streaky bacon, chopped
- 200g/7oz shallots, peeled & chopped
- 2 medium potatoes, peeled & quartered
- A few sprigs thyme
- 250ml/1 cup gluten free white wine
- 500ml/2 cups hot chicken stock
- Squeeze of lemon juice
- 2 tbsp tarragon, chopped
- Salt and pepper

1 Heat the oil in a large saucepan on a high heat and brown the chicken thighs for about 10 minutes, until they are golden. Remove them and set aside. Reduce the heat, add the bacon and shallots to the pan and gently sauté for a few minutes.

2 Add everything to the slow cooker, except the lemon juice and 1 tbsp tarragon. Cover and cook on High for 4-6 hours or until the chicken is really tender and falling off the bone.

3 Sprinkle in the lemon juice and remaining tarragon. Season with salt and pepper, and serve.

If you prefer not to use alcohol, this recipe is still tasty without the wine!

MOROCCAN LAMB SHANKS

SERVES 6 CALORIES PER SERVING 496

- 3 tsp extra-virgin olive oil
- 1¼kg/2¾lb lamb shanks
- 1 large onion, chopped
- 2 cloves garlic, crushed
- 1¼ tsp sea salt
- 1 tsp saffron threads
- ¾ tsp cinnamon
- ½ tsp cayenne pepper
- 500ml/2 cups water
- 400g/14oz tin chopped tomatoes
- 400g/14oz tin chickpeas, drained
- 1 tbsp honey
- 1 tbsp chopped flat leaf parsley

1 Heat 1 tsp oil in a large pan over medium heat. Add the lamb shanks to the pan and brown on all sides for a minute or two. Put the lamb to one side.

2 Add the remaining oil to the pan and gently sauté the onion, garlic and salt for a few minutes until softened. Stir in the saffron, cinnamon and cayenne pepper. Add water and bring to the boil.

3 Add everything to the slow cooker. Cover and cook on Low for 6-7 hours or until the lamb is cooked through and tender.

4 At the end of cooking you can shred the lamb off the bone and then stir back into the stew before serving.

Serve with rice or salad and lemon wedges.

CHICKEN, HAM AND BEAN STEW

SERVES 6 CALORIES PER SERVING 298

- 1 onion, chopped
- 225g/8oz haricot beans, rinsed
- 225g/8oz boneless, skinless chicken thighs, cubed
- 175g/6oz ham, cubed
- 1 tsp dried mixed herbs
- ½ tsp ground black pepper
- ¼ tsp nutmeg
- 1lt/4 cups gluten free hot chicken stock
- 150g/5oz kale, roughly chopped
- 1 tbsp fresh sage, chopped
- 3 tsp lemon juice
- ½ tsp salt
- 1 tbsp chopped flat leaf parsley

1 Add the onions, beans, chicken, ham, dried herbs, pepper and nutmeg into the slow cooker. Pour in the stock, combine well, cover and cook on Low for 7-8 hours.

2 When there is about an hour of cooking time remaining, stir in the kale, sage, lemon juice and salt. Cover and leave to finish cooking. Garnish with parsley before serving.

Use spinach or spring greens in the place of kale if you wish.

SMOKED HADDOCK CHOWDER

SERVES 4 CALORIES PER SERVING 315

- Knob of butter
- 3 rashers of streaky bacon, chopped
- 1½ onions, finely sliced
- 750ml/3 cups milk
- 5 medium potatoes, peeled & finely chopped
- 400g/14oz boneless smoked haddock fillets
- 200g/7oz sweetcorn
- 1 tbsp chopped flat leaf parsley

1 Heat the butter in a frying pan and sauté the bacon, potatoes and onions for a few minutes until the onions are soft.

2 Add to the slow cooker along with milk and cook on High for about an hour.

3 Stir in the sweetcorn and lay the fish on top. Cover and cook for another 25 minutes, or until the fish is cooked through and flakes easily. Sprinkle chopped parsley over the top and serve.

Add stock to alter the consistency.

SEAFOOD STEW

SERVES 6 CALORIES PER SERVING 210

- 1 tbsp olive oil
- 2 cloves garlic, crushed
- 150g/5oz carrots, finely chopped
- 600g/1lb5oz fresh tomatoes, sliced
- 1 green pepper, seeded & chopped
- ½ tsp fennel seeds
- 500ml/2 cups gluten free hot fish or chicken stock
- 450g/1lb cod fillets, cubed
- 225g/8oz king prawns, peeled
- 1 tsp dried basil
- 1 tsp brown sugar
- ½ tsp salt
- Few drops Tabasco sauce
- 2 tbsp chopped fresh flat leaf parsley

1 Mix the oil and garlic in the slow cooker. Add the carrots, tomatoes, peppers, fennel seeds & stock.

2 Combine well, cover and cook on Low for 4 hours, or until the vegetables are tender.

3 About 20 minutes before the end of cooking time, gently stir in the cod, prawns, sugar, basil, salt, and Tabasco. Cover again, and cook on High for 20-30 minutes or until the seafood is cooked through.

4 Sprinkle with parsley and serve.

Although Tabasco sauce contains vinegar there is no detectable gluten in the finished product.

SALMON WITH SPINACH

SERVES 4 CALORIES PER SERVING 267

- 350g/12oz fresh spinach
- 675g/1½lb salmon
- Salt and pepper to taste
- 2 tsp ground dill
- 2 lemons, sliced
- 60ml/¼ cup gluten free hot fish stock

1 Add the spinach to the slow cooker. Place the salmon on top, sprinkled on each side with the salt, pepper and dill.

2 Place the sliced lemons over the top of the fish and add the stock.

3 Cook on Low for 2 hours, or until the fish is cooked through and flakes easily with a fork.

Serve with a green salad or boiled new potatoes.

SUPER EASY PESTO SOLE

SERVES 4 CALORIES PER SERVING 323

- 675g/1½lb sole fillets
- 150g/5oz pesto
- 1 tbsp Parmesan cheese, grated

1 Line the inside of the slow cooker with tin foil leaving enough overhang to cover the fish.

2 Place the sole fillets in the middle, spread the pesto over the top of each and sprinkle on a little grated Parmesan. Fold the foil over and turn the edges to make a parcel.

3 Cover and cook on Low for 3-4 hours. Check the fish after 3 hours. When it is fully white and flakes easily with a fork, it is ready.

Buy labelled gluten free Pesto to ensure you are safe from cross contamination.

CHEESY PASTA

SERVES 6 · CALORIES PER SERVING 301

- 250ml/1 cup skimmed milk
- 2 egg whites
- 2 tsp cornstarch
- 125g/4oz low fat mature Cheddar cheese
- 300g/11oz gluten free pasta, preferably penne

1 Whisk together the milk, egg whites & cornstarch and add these to the slow cooker along with the cheese and pasta.

2 Cook on Low for 1½-2 hours or until the pasta is tender.

3 Stir occasionally and serve.

Gluten free pasta is generally made from rice and maize flours.

MUSHROOM PILAF

SERVES 4 · CALORIES PER SERVING 270

- 225g/8oz rice
- ½ tbsp olive oil
- 500ml/2 cups gluten free hot vegetable stock
- 4 shallots, finely chopped
- 250g/9oz mushrooms, sliced
- 1 clove garlic, crushed
- ½ tbsp fresh rosemary, chopped
- ½ tbsp fresh sage, chopped
- 1 tsp fresh thyme, chopped

1 Gently combine the rice and olive oil together in the slow cooker until the rice is coated with the oil.

2 Add the stock, shallots, mushrooms, garlic, and herbs.

3 Stir well, cover and cook on Low for 5 hours or until the rice is tender and the stock has been absorbed.

You may need to increase/decrease the amount of stock you use to get the consistency right.

CORIANDER CHICKEN

- SERVES 6
- CALORIES PER SERVING 270

- 2 x 225g/8oz jars salsa
- Juice of 1 fresh lime, halved and squeezed
- 1 tbsp taco seasoning
- 3 tbsp fresh coriander, chopped
- 1.35kg/3lbs chicken breasts, halved lengthwise

1 In your slow cooker, mix together the salsa, lime juice, taco seasoning and coriander. Drop in the chicken breasts and coat them with the salsa mixture.

2 Cover, and cook on High for about 4 hours, or on Low for 6-8 hours, until the chicken is very tender.

3 Once cooked, use 2 forks to shred the chicken.

4 Serve hot with steamed rice, garnished with fresh slices of lime or slivers of red chilli.

Reserve a little fresh coriander to sprinkle on top when serving.

HOISIN CHICKEN

- SERVES 6
- CALORIES PER SERVING 363

- Non-stick vegetable cooking spray
- 1.5kg/3½lbs chicken thighs, skinned
- Salt & pepper
- 120ml/½ cup hoisin sauce
- 225g/8oz fresh broccoli, broken into small florets
- 225g/8oz fresh carrots, peeled & sliced diagonally
- 200g/7oz cooked rice

1 Spray your slow cooker with non-stick oil. Add the chicken thighs. Season well with salt and pepper and pour the hoisin sauce over the top.

2 Cover and cook on Low for 5 hours or on High for 2½ hours.

3 Stir in the broccoli and carrots. Cook on High for another 30-40 minutes.

4 Stir in the cooked rice. Heat covered for another few minutes, and then serve hot in warmed Chinese-style bowls.

For speed, substitute a frozen mix of vegetables for the fresh broccoli and carrots.

PULLED CIDER CHICKEN

- SERVES 6
- CALORIES PER SERVING 421

- 900g/2lb skinless chicken breasts or thighs
- 2 eating apples, cored & chopped
- 1 onion, peeled & finely sliced
- 1 tsp salt
- 1 tsp garlic powder
- 250ml/1 cup cider

1 Add the apples and onions to your slow cooker. Season with ½ tsp salt.

2 Sprinkle the chicken with the remaining salt and the garlic powder. Add them to the slow cooker on top of the onion and apples. Pour about ¾ of the cider over the top.

3 Cover and cook on High for 4 hours or on Low for 6, until the chicken is very tender.

4 Remove the chicken to a chopping board and shred it, using two forks. Return it to the slow cooker, and stir in the rest of the cider.

5 Adjust the seasoning or add more cider to taste and serve.

Use dry or sweet cider according to your taste.

SIMPLE BEEF STEW

- SERVES 6
- CALORIES PER SERVING 325

- 675g/1½lb stewing steak, cubed
- 2 tbsp plain flour
- ½ tsp salt
- ¼ tsp freshly ground black pepper
- Non-stick cooking oil spray
- 1 medium onion, peeled & sliced
- 1 stalk celery, sliced
- 450g/1lb tomato passata/sieved tomatoes

1 On a plate, mix together the flour, salt and pepper, and lightly coat the steak pieces in the mixture.

2 Spray your slow cooker with non-stick oil. Add the onion, floured steak, celery and passata.

3 Cover and cook on Low for 8 hours or until the meat is very tender.

4 Serve on warmed plates or bowls, garnished with sprigs of freshly picked rosemary. Mop up the juices with some fresh crusty bread.

Stewing steak needs a long, slow cook, so this recipe always works best using the Low heat setting.

CRANBERRY BRISKET

- SERVES 6
- CALORIES PER SERVING 349

- Non-stick cooking oil spray
- 1.1kg/2½lb boneless beef brisket
- Salt & freshly ground black pepper
- 400g/14oz cranberry sauce
- 250g/8oz passata/sieved tomatoes
- 1 onion, peeled & chopped
- 1 tbsp mustard

1 Spray the inside of your slow cooker with non-stick oil.

2 Rub the brisket all over with plenty of salt and pepper, and place it in the slow cooker.

3 In a bowl, mix together the cranberry sauce, passata, onion and mustard. Pour it over the meat.

4 Cover and cook on Low for 8-10 hours or until the brisket is very tender.

5 Remove the meat from the slow cooker to a serving plate or chopping board. Slice it across the grain.

6 With a spoon, skim the fat from cooking juices and discard. To serve, pour the remaining juices over the brisket.

7 Optional serving suggestion: Enjoy with boiled new potatoes and steamed greens.

The Cranberry sauce adds sweetness to this lovely beef cut.

PULLED BEEF SANDWICHES

- SERVES 8
- CALORIES PER SERVING 575

- Non-stick cooking oil spray
- 1.35kg/3lb boneless brisket or silverside beef
- 2-3 tbsp chilli seasoning mix
- 120ml/½ cup barbecue sauce
- 8 bread rolls, split
- 8 slices Cheddar cheese

1 Spray the inside of your slow cooker with non-stick oil.

2 Cut the beef in half and place it in the slow cooker. Sprinkle it all over with chilli seasoning. Pour on the barbecue sauce.

3 Cover and cook on Low for 8-10 hours, or until the beef is very tender.

4 Remove the meat to a chopping board and allow to cool a little. Using two forks, shred the beef. Skim the fat from cooking juices with a spoon, then return the shredded beef to the slow cooker. Cover and leave to warm for another few minutes.

5 Split the bread rolls and use a slotted spoon to dollop the meat mixture into each one. Add a slice of cheese to each, close your sandwiches and enjoy with a fresh crispy salad on the side.

This is a delicious (and messy) eating experience the whole family will enjoy.

BEEF BURRITOS

- SERVES 6
- CALORIES PER SERVING 424

- 900g/2lb boneless silverside, cut in half
- Non-stick cooking oil spray
- 1 onion, peeled & chopped
- 2 cloves garlic, crushed
- 1 -2 tbsp taco seasoning
- 1 tbsp balsamic vinegar

1 Spray the inside of your slow cooker with non-stick oil.

2 Add the onion and garlic to the slow cooker. Rub the two silverside pieces with the taco seasoning and place them on top of the onion. Drizzle the balsamic vinegar over everything.

3 Cover and cook on Low for 8 hours. Shred the beef, using two forks.

4 Optional serving suggestion: Serve hot with tortillas, and top with slices of avocado and tomato and a light sprinkling of cheese.

Substitute pork shoulder for beef – it's equally delicious.

FRUITY PORK CHOPS

- SERVES 6
- CALORIES PER SERVING 454

- Non-stick cooking oil spray
- 6 boneless pork loin chops, fat trimmed
- Salt and freshly ground black pepper
- 1 tbsp freshly picked thyme leaves
- 400g/14oz dried mixed fruits, e.g. prunes and apricots
- 1 red pepper, de-seeded & sliced
- 250ml/1 cup barbecue sauce

1 Spray the inside of your slow cooker with non-stick oil. Place the chops in the bottom and season with salt and pepper. Sprinkle them with the thyme. Add the dried fruit and peppers, then pour the barbecue sauce over the top.

2 Cover and cook on Low for 4½-5 hours or on High for 2½-3.

3 Remove the chops to a serving plate. Skim the fat from sauce and discard. Spoon the sauce over the chops.

4 Optional serving suggestion: Serve hot, with new potatoes and crunchy salad. Garnish with fresh sprigs of thyme.

Dried fruit cooks wonderfully in the slow cooker, growing plump and flavoursome!

GLAZED APRICOT PORK

- SERVES 6
- CALORIES PER SERVING 596

- 1.1kg/2½lb boneless pork loin
- Non-stick cooking oil spray
- 250ml/1 cup chicken stock
- 200g/7oz apricot jam
- 2 onions, peeled & finely chopped
- 1 tbsp Dijon mustard

1. Spray the inside of your slow cooker with non-stick oil.
2. In a bowl, mix together the stock, jam, onion, and mustard.
3. Place the pork into the slow cooker and pour the stock mix over it.
4. Cover and cook on Low for 6 hours, or on High 3-3½ , or until the meat is tender.
5. Optional serving suggestion: Serve hot on pre-warmed plates, over rice.

Feel free to substitute other fruit preserves for the apricot.

EASY HAWAIIAN PORK CHOPS

- SERVES 4
- CALORIES PER SERVING 387

- 4 boneless pork chops, fat trimmed
- 400g/14oz tinned pineapple chunks in juice
- 1 tbsp brown sugar
- ½ tsp chilli flakes
- 1 tbsp soy sauce
- Salt and freshly ground black pepper

1. Pour the whole tin of pineapple into your slow cooker. Stir in the sugar, chilli flakes and soy sauce. Place the chops on top and season well with salt and pepper.
2. Cover and cook on Low for 6-8 hours or until the meat is tender.
3. Optional serving suggestion: Serve hot over rice with a crunchy green salad on the side.

You can also use a fresh pineapple. Juice half of it and add the juice to the slow cooker with the rest cut into chunks.

ITALIAN ROAST PORK

SERVES 6 · CALORIES PER SERVING 392

- 900g/2lb boneless rolled pork
- Non-stick cooking spray
- 1 large onion, peeled & roughly chopped
- 2 tsp Italian salad dressing
- 1 red pepper, de-seeded and chopped
- 60ml/¼ cup water
- 1 courgette, sliced

1 Spray the inside of your slow cooker with non-stick oil, then add the onions.

2 Rub the Italian salad dressing mix evenly over the pork. Place it in the slow cooker with the onion. Add the pepper and water.

3 Cover and cook on Low for 8 hours, or on High for 5 hours.

4 Add in the courgette, re-cover and cook for another 30 minutes or until the courgette is tender. Remove the meat and the vegetables using a slotted spoon. Skim and discard the fat from the cooking juices and keep warm.

5 Slice the meat and serve it with the vegetables on pre-warmed plates. Spoon some cooking liquid over everything to serve.

This is great served with boiled potatoes and fresh basil.

APRICOT LAMB CHOPS

SERVES 4 · CALORIES PER SERVING 585

- Non-stick cooking spray
- 4 medium lamb chops
- 4 cloves garlic, peeled & crushed
- 375g/13oz dried apricots, chopped
- 3 tbsp Dijon mustard
- 250ml/1 cup red wine

1 Spray the inside of your slow cooker with non-stick oil.

2 Place the lamb chops in the bottom of the slow cooker.

3 In a small bowl, stir together the garlic, apricots, and mustard. Spread the mixture all over the chops, then pour the red wine over the top.

4 Cover and cook on Low for about 8 hours or on High for 5, until the chops are very tender.

5 Garnish with sprigs of rosemary.

6 Optional serving suggestion: Serve hot on pre-warmed plates, with creamy mashed potato and leafy green vegetables.

For a stronger mustard flavour, use English mustard instead of Dijon.

ANCHOVY ROASTED LAMB

SERVES 6 CALORIES PER SERVING 581

- 900g/2lb boneless leg of lamb
- Non-stick cooking spray
- 100g/3½oz jar anchovies in olive oil
- 4 cloves garlic, peeled
- 1 tbsp mint sauce
- 4 medium potatoes, unpeeled & cut into wedges
- Salt & freshly ground black pepper

1 Spray the inside of your slow cooker with non-stick oil.

2 Empty the jar of anchovies into a food processor. Add the garlic and the mint sauce and blend to a smooth paste. Spread the paste all over the lamb.

3 Arrange the potato slices on the bottom of the slow cooker, and place the lamb on top.

4 Cover and cook on Low for 8 hours, or on High for 4 or 5 or until the lamb is tender all the way through.

5 Serve with sprigs of fresh mint.

6 Optional serving suggestion: Add a side serving of baby carrots.

Anchovies add depth of flavour to this tasty meal!

PESTO SOLE

SERVES 6 CALORIES PER SERVING 198

- 900g/2lb fresh Dover sole fillets
- 2 tbsp pesto
- 2 tsp Parmesan cheese, grated
- 2 courgettes, sliced
- 4 spears fresh asparagus

1 Spread out a small sheet of foil. Place a piece of fish on it. Spread on a teaspoon of pesto. Add a couple of slices of courgette and an asparagus spear then sprinkle a little Parmesan over the top.

2 Fold over the foil to make a parcel and put it in your slow cooker. Repeat with each fillet

3 Cover and cook on Low for 2-3 hours until the fish flakes against a fork.

4 Unwrap the parcels carefully and serve immediately with crusty bread to mop up the juices.

Lemon sole will work too if you can't get Dover sole.

TROUT IN WHITE WINE

SERVES 4 CALORIES PER SERVING 352

- Non-stick cooking spray
- 4 fresh medium whole trout, gutted & headed
- 125g/4oz mushrooms, sliced
- 180ml/¾ cup white wine
- Juice & grated rind of 1 lemon
- Salt & freshly ground black pepper
- 120ml/½ cup creme fraiche

1 Spray the inside of your slow cooker with non-stick oil.

2 Arrange the trout in the slow cooker. Add the mushrooms, wine, and the lemon rind and juice. Season with salt and pepper.

3 Cover and cook on Low for 3 to 4 hours.

4 Stir in the creme fraiche and heat a further 15 minutes or so.

5 Optional serving suggestion: Serve warm with new potatoes, and steamed fresh green vegetables.

It's easy to overcook fish, so to be safe, check it after 2 hours. Slow cookers may vary!

COD IN TOMATO SAUCE

SERVES 4 CALORIES PER SERVING 168

- 4 cod steaks (each weighing 150g/5oz each)
- 400g/14oz tinned chopped tomatoes with garlic
- 1 tbsp tomato puree
- Salt & freshly ground black pepper
- 1 green pepper, de-seeded & diced
- 1 onion, peeled & finely chopped

1 In a bowl, stir together the chopped tomatoes and tomato puree. Season with salt and pepper. Stir in the green pepper and onion.

2 Place the fish steaks in your slow cooker and pour the tomato sauce over the top.

3 Cover and cook on Low for 2 to 3 hours, or on High for around 1-2.

4 Serve with slices of fresh tomato and cucumber. Garnish with torn fresh basil leaves.

For this recipe, you can substitute any firm white fish for the cod.

THAI SHRIMP CURRY

SERVES 4 CALORIES PER SERVING 386

- 750ml/3 cups light coconut milk
- 120ml/½ cup Thai red curry paste
- 2½ tsp lemon pepper seasoning
- 1 tbsp fresh coriander, chopped
- 600g/1lb 5oz king prawns, with shells

1 Pour the coconut milk into your slow cooker. Stir in the red curry paste, lemon pepper and half the coriander.

2 Cover and cook on High for 2 hours.

3 Add the shrimp and the rest of the coriander, re-cover and cook for a further 20-30 minutes or until the shrimp are cooked.

4 Serve hot over brown rice or couscous, garnished with fresh coriander leaves, desiccated coconut and a spoonful of natural yogurt.

Test the shrimp frequently after 10 minutes cooking – you may find they cook faster than expected.

STUFFED PEPPERS

SERVES 4 CALORIES PER SERVING 379

- 4 fresh peppers, any colour will do
- 400g/14oz tinned baked beans with chilli
- 250g/8oz cooked rice
- 225g/4oz Cheddar cheese, grated
- Salt & freshly ground black pepper
- 400g/14oz passata/sieved tomatoes

1 Cut the tops off the peppers and de-seed them. Reserve the tops.

2 In a bowl, stir together the chilli beans, rice, and half of the cheese. Season with salt and pepper. Spoon the mixture into the peppers and replace the tops.

3 Pour the passata into your slow cooker. Place the filled peppers in the sauce.

4 Cover and cook on Low for 6-6½ hours or on High for 3-3½.

5 Transfer the peppers to a serving plate. Spoon the tomato sauce over the peppers and scatter the remaining cheese on top.

Instead of chilli beans, try with chickpeas and a couple of cloves of crushed garlic.

LINGUINE WITH ARTICHOKE

SERVES 5 CALORIES PER SERVING 408

- Non-stick cooking spray
- 2 x 400g/14oz tinned chopped tomatoes with garlic
- 2 x 400g/14oz cans artichoke hearts, drained & quartered
- 6 cloves garlic, peeled & crushed
- 120ml/½ cup double cream
- 350g/12oz dried linguine

1 Spray the inside of your slow cooker with non-stick oil.

2 Pour the chopped tomatoes into the slow cooker. Add the artichoke hearts and the garlic.

3 Cover and cook on Low for 6-8 hours or on High for 3-4 hours.

4 Stir in the cream and leave to heat through for about 5 minutes.

5 Cook the pasta separately, according to the packet instructions, and drain.

6 Serve the sauce over the pasta in pre-warmed bowls. Garnish with olives and Parmesan cheese.

To lower the calorie count a little more, use crème fraiche or low fat natural yogurt instead of double cream.

CAJUN VEGETABLE CASSEROLE

SERVES 6 CALORIES PER SERVING 151

- 2 x 400g/14oz tinned black beans, rinsed & drained
- 2 x 400g/14oz tinned tomatoes
- 2 onions, peeled & chopped
- 1 tbsp Cajun seasoning

1 In your slow cooker stir together the beans, tomatoes, onions and Cajun seasoning.

2 Cover and cook on Low for 6-8 hours or on High for 3-4 hours.

3 Optional serving suggestion: Serve hot over cooked brown rice and scatter with torn basil leaves.

Feel free to vary the vegetables you use according to what you have in your kitchen.

LENTIL CURRY

SERVES 6 · CALORIES PER SERVING 365

- 400g/14oz green lentils, uncooked, well-rinsed
- 1 tsp coconut oil
- 1 onion, finely chopped
- 6 cloves garlic, peeled & crushed
- 1 tbsp curry powder
- Salt & freshly ground black pepper
- 400g/14oz light coconut milk
- 750ml/3 cups boiling water

1 Heat the coconut oil in a small pan. Add the onion and garlic and cook gently for about 5 minutes, stirring occasionally. Add the curry powder, salt and pepper and stir for another half minute or so.

2 Scrape the mixture into your slow cooker. Stir in the coconut milk, lentils and water.

3 Cover and cook on Low for 7-8 hours or on High for about 4.

4 Garnish with chopped fresh coriander leaves and spring onions.

5 Optional serving suggestion: Serve over brown rice or couscous.

You can store leftovers in the fridge for up to 3 days, or in the freezer for up to 3 months in an airtight container.

MACARONI CHEESE

SERVES 4 · CALORIES PER SERVING 538

- 1 tbsp butter, diced
- 300g/11oz dried macaroni
- 225g/8oz mature Cheddar cheese, grated
- 125g/4oz Gruyere cheese, grated
- 500ml/2 cups semi-skimmed milk
- Salt & freshly ground black pepper

1 Drop the butter into your slow cooker. Tip in the macaroni and stir to coat the pasta. Stir in both varieties of cheese and pour in the milk. Season well, then stir everything up.

2 Cover and cook on Low for about 5 hours, stirring occasionally until the pasta is tender.

3 Serve hot in pre-warmed pasta bowls, garnished with fresh basil and parsley, and sprinkled with Parmesan and more black pepper. Enjoy with a crunchy salad on the side, or as an accompaniment to another dish.

Vary your cheeses to find the combination you like best.

BROCCOLI & TORTELLINI MARINARA

SERVES 4   CALORIES PER SERVING 375

- 750g/1lb 11oz jar marinara pasta sauce
- 60ml/¼ cup water
- 1 tbsp fresh basil leaves, torn
- 1 tbsp fresh oregano, chopped
- Salt and freshly ground black pepper
- 250g/9oz pre-packed spinach and cheese tortellini
- 450g/1lb fresh broccoli, broken into florets

1 In a bowl, combine the marinara sauce, water basil and oregano. Season well with salt and pepper.

2 Pour about a third of the sauce into your slow cooker, then tip in the tortellini. Pour half the remaining sauce over the tortellini. Distribute the broccoli over the top and pour on the remaining sauce.

3 Cover and cook on High for 2-2½ hours, until the broccoli and pasta are tender but not mushy.

4 Serve hot in pasta bowls, with slices of ripe tomato and freshly picked parsley and basil to garnish.

Use a different pasta sauce if you prefer. For best results make your own, but for ease, there are several varieties readily available in supermarkets.

AUBERGINE RAGU

SERVES 4   CALORIES PER SERVING 226

- 2 tbsp olive oil
- 1 large onion, peeled & chopped
- 1 large aubergine, peeled, cut into 1-inch pieces
- Salt and freshly ground black pepper
- 5 cloves garlic, peeled & crushed
- 2 x 400g/14oz tinned tomatoes
- 7g/¼oz fresh basil leaves, torn

1 Pour the oil into your slow cooker. Tip in the onion and aubergine and season with salt and pepper. Stir everything up to coat the vegetables.

2 Stir in the garlic, tomatoes and basil.

3 Cover and cook on Low for 4-5 hours or on High for 3, until the aubergine is tender.

4 Garnish with fresh basil leaves and grated Parmesan.

5 Optional serving suggestion: Serve over brown rice , pasta or polenta.

Use this basic recipe with any vegetables you like, for example carrots and courgettes.

SPANISH TORTILLA

- SERVES 4
- CALORIES PER SERVING 396

- A dozen eggs, gently fork-whisked
- One large onion, chopped
- 150g/5oz potatoes, peeled and cut into thin slices
- 50g/2oz cured chorizo Spanish sausage, finely chopped
- Low cal cooking spray
- Salt & pepper to taste

1 Gently sauté the onions and potatoes in a little low cal spray until golden (5-10 mins). Spray the slow cooker with a little more oil and add all the ingredients.

2 Combine well, cover and leave to cook on low overnight for 6-8 hours for a perfect morning feast.

This Spanish omelette makes a fantastic hearty start to the morning. It's also great served cold and cut into slices with a fresh green salad.

BEAN, ROSEMARY & GARLIC DIP

- SERVES 14
- CALORIES PER SERVING 88

- 6 garlic cloves chopped
- 100g/3½ oz parmesan cheese grated
- 1 bunch chopped fresh rosemary
- 2 tbsp extra virgin olive oil
- 1 400g/14oz tin borlotti beans, drained
- 125g/4oz low fat cream cheese
- Handful chopped black olives
- 1 tbsp white wine vinegar
- 250ml/1 cup water
- 1 tbsp lemon juice
- Salt to taste

1 Quickly pulse all the ingredients (except the lemon juice) in a food processor. Empty the blitzed mixture into the slow cooker and leave to cook on low for 1-2 hours. If the mixture is too thick, add a little more water. If it's not thick enough, continue to cook with the lid off until you get the required consistency.

2 After cooking allow to cool, stir in the lemon juice and serve with a selection of raw celery, cucumber and carrot batons.

This is a perfect low cal snack to keep you going between meals.

NACHO BEAN & ONION DIP

SERVES 12 · CALORIES PER SERVING 90

- 2 400g/14oz tins low fat refried beans
- 1 green chilli, finely chopped
- 1 onion, chopped
- 100g/3½ oz mozzarella cheese chopped
- 250ml/1 cup water
- Salt to taste
- 1 tbsp lemon juice
- 4 tsp taco seasoning mix
- Or make your own:
- 2 tsp mild chilli powder, 1 ½ tsp ground cumin, ½ tsp paprika, ¼ tsp each of onion powder, garlic powder, dried oregano & crushed chilli flakes, 1 tsp each of sea salt & black pepper

1 Place all the ingredients, except the lemon juice, into the slow cooker and combine well.

2 Leave to cook on low for 1-2 hours and before serving, stir in the lemon juice. If the mixture is too thick add a little more water. If it's not thick enough, continue to cook with the lid off until you get the required consistency.

3 Serve warm with plain tortilla chips.

Buffallo mozzarella is good in this recipe but regular mozzarella is fine too. Use the full fat versions of both.

HONEY ROASTED VEGETABLES

SERVES 6 · CALORIES PER SERVING 281

- 250g/9oz carrots
- 250g/9oz parsnips
- 1 tbsp balsamic vinegar
- 3 tsp runny honey
- 2 red onions
- 2 red (bell) peppers
- 2 tbsp olive oil
- 1 tsp each ground cumin, paprika, & chilli powder
- ½ tsp ground cinnamon
- 200g/7oz tinned chopped tomatoes
- Salt & pepper to taste

1 Peel and cut the carrots, parsnips, peppers and onions into chunks.

2 Combine all the ingredients well in the slow cooker. Season, cover and leave to cook on low for 3-4 hours or until the vegetables are tender. Add a little water during cooking if needed.

This is a great Moroccan inspired dish which is also nice with some chopped apricots if you like additional sweetness.

FRESH CHERRY & ALMONDS

SERVES 4 CALORIES PER SERVING 260

- 800g/1¾lb cherries, deseeded
- 100g/3½oz brown sugar
- 60ml/¼ cup boiling water
- 3 tbsp chopped almonds
- ½ tsp vanilla extract

1 Place all the ingredients in the slow cooker.

2 Cover and leave to cook on high for 1-2 hours or until the cherries are tender and syrupy.

3 Allow to cool and serve (sprinkle with a little more brown sugar if needed).

June is a wonderful month for fresh cherries. This dish is lovely served with low fat crème fraiche.

SLOW COOKED SALSA

SERVES 4 CALORIES PER SERVING 30

- 1kg/2¼lb ripe tomatoes, chopped
- 6 garlic cloves, crushed
- 2 onions, chopped (reserve 1 onion)
- ½ tsp each ground cumin & coriander
- 2 red chillies, finely chopped
- 250ml/1 cup passata/sieved tomatoes
- 1 tsp brown sugar
- 2 tbsp freshly chopped coriander

1 Place the tomatoes, garlic, onion, cumin, ground coriander, chopped chillies, passata and sugar in the slow cooker. Cover and leave to cook on low for 4-5 hours or until the tomatoes have broken down and are super tender.

2 Place in a food processor and pulse a few times.

3 Stir through the reserved fresh onion to give the salsa a crunch and garnish with the freshly chopped coriander.

4 Chill and serve.

Adjust the chilli to suit your own taste and serve as a fresh side to BBQ meats or with tortilla chips.

CINNAMON STEWED APRICOTS

SERVES 4 · CALORIES PER SERVING 155

- 12 ripe apricots, stoned & halved
- 125g/4oz brown sugar (reserve ½ tsp of sugar)
- ½ tsp vanilla extract
- ½ tsp ground cinnamon
- 250ml/1 cup water

1 Stone and halve the fresh apricots. Place all the ingredients in the slow cooker.

2 Combine well, cover and leave to cook on low for 4-6 hours or until the apricots are tender.

3 Sprinkle with the reserved brown sugar and serve.

Late summer is the best month for domestic apricots. Enjoy these just as they are or with a little fresh ice cream.

SEASONAL POACHED STRAWBERRIES

SERVES 4 · CALORIES PER SERVING 125

- 800g/1¾lb hulled ripe strawberries
- 75g/3oz brown sugar
- 60ml/¼ cup water
- 2 tbsp lemon juice

1 Place all the ingredients in the slow cooker.

2 Combine well, cover and leave to cook on high for 1-2 hours or until the strawberries are tender but not falling apart.

3 Check the balance of the sweetness and serve.

The first strawberries of the year are a welcome sight. Their natural sweetness is far superior to the 'forced' fruit that is available all year round.

LATE SUMMER PLUMS

SERVES 4 CALORIES PER SERVING 140

- 800g/1¾lb plums, halved & deseeded
- 75g/3oz brown sugar
- 1 tbsp runny honey
- 2 tsp balsamic vinegar
- 250ml/1 cup boiling water
- 1 tbsp lemon juice

1 Place all the ingredients in the slow cooker.

2 Combine well, cover and leave to cook on high for 2-3 hours or until the plums are tender.

3 Spoon the plums out of the slow cooker along with as much syrup as you wish.

4 Check the balance of the sweetness and serve.

Late summer is when plums are harvested. Don't worry if they are not very ripe, this recipe will work well anyway.

POACHED AUGUST PEARS

SERVES 4 CALORIES PER SERVING 120

- 4 ripe pears
- 250ml/1 cup fresh orange juice
- 75g/3oz brown sugar
- 60ml/¼ cup boiling water
- ½ tsp vanilla extract

1 Peel, core and halve the pears. Place all the ingredients in the slow cooker.

2 Combine well, cover and leave to cook on high for 1-2 hours or until the pears are tender.

3 Serve whilst warm with the juice spooned over the top.

August is the first month domestic pears really come into season. Use the ripest pears you can get your hands on & serve with fat free Greek yoghurt if you like.

FRUIT GRANOLA

SERVES 4 CALORIES PER SERVING 300

- 500g/1lb 2oz plain granola cereal
- 100g/3 ½ oz oatmeal
- 1 tsp cinnamon
- ½ tsp nutmeg
- 1 tbsp runny honey
- 4 apples sliced & cored
- 50g/2oz sultanas
- 50g/2oz low fat 'butter' spread, melted

1 Add all the ingredients to the slow cooker and combine well. Cover and leave to cook for 2-3 hours making sure the granola doesn't burn. Serve with milk if you like.

Add all the ingredients to the slow cooker and combine well. Cover and leave to cook for 2-3 hours making sure the granola doesn't burn. Serve with milk if you like.

MORNING RISOTTO

SERVES 4 CALORIES PER SERVING 271

- 175g/6oz risotto rice
- 4 apples, peeled, cored & sliced
- 125g/4oz sultanas
- 1 tsp cinnamon
- ½ tsp nutmeg
- ¼ tsp ground cloves
- 500ml/2 cups water
- 500ml/2 cups skimmed milk
- 1 tbsp brown sugar
- Knob butter

1 Melt the butter in a pan and add the rice. Make sure it's all nicely coated for just a minute or two and then add all the ingredients to the slow cooker.

2 Leave to cook overnight for 6-8 hours with the lid tightly closed. If it feels a little stodgy in the morning loosen it up by stirring a dash of cold milk through.

A lovely breakfast alternative or daytyime snack which uses Italian rice to give the dish its base.

WARMING SPICED APPLES

SERVES 4 • CALORIES PER SERVING 300

- 4 medium cooking apples
- 125g/4oz raisins & sultanas
- 75g/3oz brown sugar
- ½ teaspoon each of nutmeg and cinnamon
- 60ml/ ¼ cup apple juice
- 50g/2 oz chopped walnuts
- 1 tbsp low fat 'butter' spread

1 Core the apples. Mix together the raisins, brown sugar, spices and 'butter' then stuff into the cored apples.

2 Add the apples to the slow cooker and pour the apple juice into the bottom. Leave to cook on a low heat with the lid tightly closed for 5-6 hours or high for 2-3 hours. Add a little water during cooking if needed.

3 Remove the apples and spoon over any liquid from the bottom of the cooker. Delicious served with ice-cream.

This lovely dessert has a hint of Christmas spice to it which will warm you to the bone.

CINNAMON APPLES

SERVES 6 • CALORIES PER SERVING 230

- 6 cooking apples peeled, cored
- and cut into wedges
- 1 tbsp lemon juice
- 75g/3oz brown sugar
- 75g/3oz raisins
- 75g/3oz chopped pecan nuts
- 125g/4oz low fat 'butter'
- spread, gently melted
- 2 tsp ground cinnamon
- 120ml/ ½ cup water
- 1 tsp cornflour

1 Coat the apple slices well with the lemon juice and then combine all the ingredients in the slow cooker.

2 Cook on low for 3 hours with the lid tightly shut or until the apples are tender.

3 Add a little more water during cooking if needed.

The aroma around your home of apple and cinnamon as they cook is wonderful. This warming dessert is even better served with a little cream or ice cream on the side.

BUCKLE BERRY COBBLER

- SERVES 4
- CALORIES PER SERVING 320

- 75g/3oz plain/all purpose flour
- 200g/7oz brown sugar
- ½ tsp baking powder
- ½ tsp ground cinnamon
- 1 egg, lightly beaten
- 120ml/ ½ cup fat-free milk
- 2 tsp olive oil
- 150g/5oz raspberries
- 150g/5oz blueberries

1 Combine the flour, sugar, baking powder and cinnamon together.

2 In a separate bowl mix together the egg, milk and oil. Gently combine both mixes together along with the fruit in the slow cooker and leave to cook on high for 2-3 hours with the lid tightly closed.

3 You can check the cobbler is ready by inserting a clean knife into the mixture. If it comes out clean it's cooked and ready to enjoy, if not leave it for a little longer.

Buckle cobbler is an old American term which means berries and batter. You can use any berries for this.

BREAD PUDDING

- SERVES 6
- CALORIES PER SERVING 330

- 5 slices cubed white bread (a
- couple of days old is best)
- 500ml/2 cups skimmed milk
- 4 free range eggs
- 1 tsp ground cinnamon
- 100g/3 ½ oz brown sugar
- 125g/4oz low fat 'butter'
- spread
- ½ tsp vanilla extract
- ¼ tsp ground nutmeg
- 150g/5oz raisins and sultanas

1 Combine all the ingredients in the slow cooker and leave to cook on low for 3-5 hours with the lid tightly shut.

2 The pudding may need a little more milk during cooking, or if it needs thickening remove the lid and leave to cook on high for a further 45 minutes or until you get the desired consistency.

This is a classic dessert recipe that everyone loves and is so easy to make. If you are feeling indulgent you could also add a handful of chocolate chips.

RICE PUDDING

SERVES 4 | CALORIES PER SERVING 170

- 100g/3 ½oz pudding rice
- ½ tsp ground cinnamon
- 50g/2oz brown sugar
- 75g/3oz raisins or sultanas
- 750ml/3 cups semi skimmed milk
- ½ tsp ground nutmeg
- 1 bayleaf
- 1 tsp low fat 'butter' spread

1 Add the rice, sugar, butter, milk and bay leaf to the slow cooker and leave to cook on high for 2-3 hours with the lid tightly closed.

2 Make sure the rice is nice and tender - you may need to add some milk during cooking if needed. Sprinkle over the nutmeg before serving and remove the bay leaf. Lovely served with a dollop of jam.

Rice pudding is a dish enjoyed by the people of almost every continent of the world. This European version was exported to the US by immigrants in the latter part of the 20th century.

CITRUS SLICE

SERVES 6 | CALORIES PER SERVING 190

- 175g/6oz low fat 'butter'
- spread
- 100g/3 ½oz brown sugar
- 75g/3oz self raising flour
- 1 tbsp of lemon or lime zest
- 6 tbsp lemon or lime juice
- 3 egg yolks
- 120ml/ ½ cup semi skimmed milk
- 4 egg whites
- 250ml/1 cup water

1 Mix together the low fat spread and sugar, add the flour and lemon juice zest. Whisk in the egg yolks and milk.

2 Beat the egg whites until they peak then fold into your cake mixture. Pour the mixture into a cake tin and cover with foil.

3 Add the water to the slow cooker and place the covered cake tin on top.

4 Cover and cook on low for 5-6 hours or until it is nicely cooked through. Serve with cream or ice cream as preferred.

A lovely citrus pudding and a real treat.

STEWED RHUBARB & CREAM

SERVES 4 · CALORIES PER SERVING 170

- 500g/1lb 2oz rhubarb, chopped
- 100g/3½ oz brown sugar
- 3 tbsp water
- 250ml/1 cup single cream

1. Place all the ingredients, except the cream, in the slow cooker and combine well.
2. Cover, season and leave to cook on low for 2-4 hours or until the rhubarb is very tender.
3. Add a little more water during cooking if needed.
4. Divide into bowls and swirl the cream over the top.

If you are lucky enough to have wild rhubarb growing locally, make use of the summer glut and freeze batches ready-stewed for later in the year.

GINGER PLUMS & GREEK YOGHURT

SERVES 4 · CALORIES PER SERVING 262

- 900g/2lb plums, halved and stoned
- 1 tbsp freshly grated ginger
- 3 tbsp runny honey
- 500ml/2 cups fat free Greek yoghurt

1. Place all the ingredients, except the yoghurt, in the slow cooker and combine well. Cover and leave to cook on low for 4-6 hours. Add a little water during cooking if needed.
2. Divide the yoghurt into bowls and serve with the plums piled on top.

Feel free to use ground ginger if you don't have any fresh to hand.

APRICOTS & PISTACHIOS

SERVES 4 | CALORIES PER SERVING 190

- 75g/3oz caster sugar
- 800g/1¾lb apricots, halved and stoned
- ½ tsp vanilla essence
- 100g/3½oz pistachios, chopped
- 120ml/½ cup water

1 Add all the ingredients, except the pistachios, into the slow cooker.

2 Cover and leave to cook on low for 2-3 hours or until the apricots are soft and the liquid syrupy.

3 Sprinkle the pistachios over the top and serve with low fat crème fraiche.

If the apricots are under- ripe you might need to add a little more sugar.

ROSEWATER APRICOTS

SERVES 4 | CALORIES PER SERVING 163

- 800g/1¾lb ripe apricots, halved & stoned
- 100g/3½oz caster sugar
- 180ml/¾ cup water
- A few drops rosewater
- 1 tbsp Greek yogurt, to serve
- 50g/2oz pistachios, roughly chopped

1 Place the apricots in your slow cooker. Sprinkle on the sugar and add the water. Cover and cook on Low for 2 hours or until the apricots are soft and cooked through.

2 Place into a clean bowl, splash in the rosewater and leave to cool. Spoon into glasses and top with a teaspoon of yoghurt, sprinkled with the chopped pistachio nuts.

Once cooled, the poached apricots can be frozen for later.

APPLE CRUMBLE

SERVES 6   CALORIES PER SERVING 447

- 1.1kg/2½lb eating apples
- 3 tbsp apricot jam
- Juice of 1 large orange

For the crumble:
- 140g/4½oz oats
- 100g/3½oz plain flour
- 1 tsp ground cinnamon
- 100g/3½oz butter
- 100g/3½oz light muscovado sugar
- 1 tbsp golden syrup

1 Peel, core and thinly slice the apples. Place them in the slow cooker and combine with the jam and orange juice.

2 Mix the crumble ingredients in a bowl using your fingers to combine well. Spread the crumble over the apples.

3 Cook on Low for 2-4 hours or until tender and cooked through.

4 Serve with your choice of cream or ice cream.

To ensure the crumble is crisp, leave the slow cooker lid slighly ajar for the last 10 minutes of cooking.

APPLE AND PEAR COMPOTE

SERVES 6   CALORIES PER SERVING 211

- 4 eating apples, peeled, cored & chopped
- 2 medium cooking apples, peeled, cored & chopped
- 4 firm pears, peeled, cored & sliced
- 100g/3½oz dried cherries
- 3 tbsp brown sugar
- 120ml/½ cup water

1 Place the apples, pears, cherries and sugar into the slow cooker.

2 Add the water and combine well. Cover and cook on Low for 8-10 hours or until and the pears and apples are tender.

3 Divide into bowls and serve.

Try using cranberries instead of cherries if you prefer.

CHOCOLATE FUDGE

SERVES 6 | CALORIES PER SERVING 190

- 225g/8oz cups chocolate chips
- 60ml/¼ cup light coconut milk
- 25g/1oz sugar
- Pinch of salt
- 1 tbsp vegetable oil
- ½ tsp pure vanilla extract

1 Add the chocolate chips, coconut milk, sugar, salt, and vegetable oil into your slow cooker. Combine everything together, cover and cook on Low for 2 hours. Do not stir during cooking.

2 After 2 hours, switch off the slow cooker. Add the vanilla, still without stirring. Leave to cool to room temperature, then stir vigorously for a minute or two.

3 Lightly oil a large dish or baking tray. Pour the fudge into pan, cover and refrigerate for 4 hours or until firm.

This could be a perfect indulgent gift for family and friends.

RICE PUDDING

SERVES 4 | CALORIES PER SERVING 320

- 150g/5oz long grain pudding rice
- 1 tsp ground cinnamon
- 50g/2oz sugar
- 380ml/1½ cups light coconut milk
- 380ml1½ cups semi-skimmed milk
- 100g/3½oz raisins
- 1 tsp pure vanilla extract

1 Add the rice, cinnamon and sugar to your slow cooker and combine well. Stir in the milk and coconut milk, cover and cook on Low for 3-4 hours or until the rice is tender.

2 Stir in the vanilla extract and raisins, and re-cover. Switch off the slow cooker and leave the pudding to set for 10-20 minutes.

3 Serve with extra cinnamon and raisins if you wish.

Since slow cookers tend to vary, check the consistency of your pudding after 3 hours and see if it needs any longer. Feel free to add more milk if required.

BANANAS AND RUM

SERVES 6 CALORIES PER SERVING 130

- 1 tbsp coconut oil
- 3 tbsp honey
- 1 tbsp lemon juice
- ¼ tsp ground cinnamon
- 6 medium bananas, peeled & sliced
- Splash of rum

1 Combine the coconut oil, honey, lemon juice and cinnamon in the slow cooker.

2 Add the banana slices, and toss gently to coat with the honey mixture.

3 Cover and cook on low for 1½ - 2 hours. Stir in a splash of rum, and serve.

If you prefer not to use alcohol you could try a splash of cider vinegar instead.

CRISPY SPICED APPLES

SERVES 4 CALORIES PER SERVING 220

- 3 eating apples, peeled, cored & diced
- 1 tbsp lemon juice
- 100g/3½oz sugar
- 50g/2oz flour
- 25g/1oz oats
- 1 tsp ground cinnamon
- ½ tsp ground nutmeg
- ¼ tsp all spice
- 2 tbsp butter
- Salt to taste

1 Spread the apples in your bottom of the slow cooker. Add the lemon juice and combine so that the apples are coated. Stir in half the sugar and the cinnamon.

2 In a small bowl, mix the flour, oats, the remaining sugar, nutmeg, all spice, and salt. Use your fingers and thumbs to rub the butter into the mixture until you create a consistency of crumbs.

3 Sprinkle the crumb mixture over the apples. Cover and cook on Low for 4 hours or until the apples are tender.

A gorgeous warming pudding...especially in winter

SPICED APPLES WITH CREAM

- SERVES 4
- CALORIES PER SERVING 135

- 4 eating apples, peeled, cored and sliced
- 2 tbsp honey
- ½ tsp ground cinnamon
- ½ tsp ground cloves
- 25g/1oz butter, sliced
- 1 tbsp low-fat whipped cream or crème fraiche

1 Tip the apples into the slow cooker and toss them with the honey, cinnamon, cloves, and butter.

2 Cover and cook on Low for 4-5 hours, or until the apples are very tender.

3 Serve with a spoonful of cream.

Be careful not to overcook your apples or they'll turn into apple sauce!

TAPIOCA PUDDING

- SERVES 4
- CALORIES PER SERVING 324

- 2 eggs
- 1lt/4 cups skimmed milk
- 150g/5oz brown sugar
- 75g/3oz pearl tapioca
- 1 tsp vanilla extract

1 Use a fork to beat the eggs in a cup.

2 Add all the ingredients to the slow cooker and mix well. Cover and cook on Low for 5-6 hours, stirring occasionally.

3 Serve warm.

Use tapioca pearls rather than powder if possible

OATS AND MAPLE SYRUP

SERVES 4 · CALORIES PER SERVING 357

- 360ml/1½ cups skimmed milk
- 360ml/1½ cups water
- Cooking spray
- 2 apples, peeled, cored & cubed
- 100g/3½oz oats
- 2 tbsp brown sugar
- 1½ tsp butter, softened
- ¼ tsp ground cinnamon
- ¼ tsp salt
- 60ml/¼ cup maple syrup
- 2 tbsp hazelnuts, chopped

1 Pour the milk and water into a pan and bring to the boil, stirring frequently.

2 Coat the slow cooker with cooking spray to prevent sticking. Pour in the hot milk mixture. Add the cubed apples, oats, sugar, butter, cinnamon and salt. Stir well. Cover and cook on Low for 7 hours or until the oats are tender.

3 Spoon into bowls, top with maple syrup and chopped hazelnuts.

Also good served with ice cream.

TROPICAL TAPIOCA

SERVES 6 · CALORIES PER SERVING 212

- Cooking spray
- 175g/6oz sugar
- 75g/3oz pearl tapioca
- 2 x 400ml/14oz tins light coconut milk
- 1 large egg
- 100g/3½oz fresh pineapple, finely chopped
- 40g/1½oz coconut flakes

1 Coat the slow cooker with cooking spray to prevent sticking. Add the sugar, tapioca & coconut milk and whisk together. Cover and cook on Low for 2 hours or until the tapioca is transparent.

2 Crack the egg into a bowl, beat with a fork and stir the egg mixture into the tapioca in the slow cooker.

3 Cover and cook on Low for 30 minutes. Switch off the slow cooker. Stir the pineapple into the tapioca mixture. Cover once more and leave to stand for 30 minutes. Serve either warm or chilled. Top each serving with the coconut flakes.

Tinned pineapple also works fine for this recipe.

SPICED APPLE CAKE

SERVES 6 CALORIES PER SERVING 238

- Cooking spray
- 100g/3½oz all-purpose flour
- 25g/1oz dark brown sugar
- ½ tsp baking soda
- 1 tsp ground cinnamon
- ¼ tsp baking powder
- Pinch salt
- Pinch ground nutmeg
- Pinch ground cloves
- 125g/4oz unsweetened apple sauce
- 60ml/¼ cup low-fat buttermilk
- 25g/1oz butter, melted
- ½ tbsp vanilla extract
- 1 small egg
- 100g/3½oz dried apple slices, coarsely chopped
- ½ tsp icing sugar (optional)

1 Coat the slow cooker with cooking spray. Line the bottom with parchment paper, lengthwise and breadthwise. Coat the parchment with cooking spray too.

2 Combine the flour, brown sugar, baking soda, cinnamon, baking powder, salt, nutmeg and cloves in a bowl. In another bowl, combine together the apple sauce, buttermilk, butter, vanilla and egg to create a sauce. Stir this sauce mixture into the flour mixture until it's smooth. Add the dried apple and combine.

3 Place the contents of the bowl into the slow cooker, spreading it into an even layer. Cover and cook on High for 1 - 1½ hours or until the cake has risen.

4 Remove the cake. Cut it into wedges and sprinkle with icing sugar.

ALMOND & RASPBERRY CHEESECAKE

SERVES 6 CALORIES PER SERVING 390

- 16 amoretti biscuits, broken into crumbs
- 2 tbsp butter, melted
- 1 tbsp sugar
- Cooking spray
- 450g/1lb fat-free cream cheese, softened and divided
- 225g/8oz reduced fat cream cheese, softened
- 150g/5oz brown sugar
- 1 tbsp plain flour
- 2 large eggs
- ¾ tsp almond extract
- A handful of fresh raspberries

1 For the crust, combine the biscuit crumbs, butter and sugar with a fork until moist. Gently press the mixture into the bottom of a 7-inch baking dish coated with cooking spray.

2 For the filling, blend together the fat free and fat-reduced cheeses. Add the sugar and flour and beat well. Add the eggs, 1 at a time, beating well after each. Stir in the almond extract. Pour the cheese mixture over the crust in the baking dish.

3 Pour the hot water into your slow cooker. Place a rack inside that is higher than the water level. Place the dish with the cheesecake on the rack, and cover with several layers of paper towels.

4 Replace the lid on the slow cooker and cook on High for 2 hours or until the middle of the cheesecake sets (it should barely move when the dish is touched). Uncover the slow cooker. Switch it off and run a knife around outside edge of the baking dish. Leave the cheesecake standing in the slow cooker for an hour and then remove it.

5 Cool to room temperature. Cover and chill for 6 hours. Cut into wedges, and top with a few rasps.

VANILLA CUSTARD

SERVES 4 CALORIES PER SERVING 195

- 2 x 170g tins evaporated low-fat milk
- 120ml/ ½ cup skimmed milk
- 1 tsp vanilla paste
- 1 large egg, lightly beaten
- 2 large egg yolks
- 75g/3oz sugar

1 Pour both kinds of milk into a saucepan. Bring to a simmer, then remove the pan from the heat and add the vanilla paste. Whisk until blended.

2 In a bowl, whisk the egg, egg yolks and sugar. Gradually add the hot milk, beating vigorously with a whisk. Pour the egg mixture through a sieve into a bowl.

3 Place 4 metal canning jar bands in the bottom of your slow cooker. Ladle the egg mixture evenly into 4 ramekins. Cover the ramekins with foil. Set 1 ramekin on each band, making sure ramekins do not touch each other or the sides of slow cooker. Pour hot water into the slow cooker to a depth of 1 inch up the sides of the ramekins.

4 Cover and cook on High for 1¾ hours, or until the custard is 'set'. Remove the ramekins from the slow cooker, and cool on a wire rack.

5 Serve warm or chilled.

Using evaporated milk should prevent the custard from curdling.

Printed in Great Britain
by Amazon

85979512R00063